Origami Birds

Origami Birds

John Montroll

Dover Publications, Inc.
New York

To Ryan, Joseph, Avery, Henry, C.J., Nino, Thomas, Conrad, Matias, and Charlie

Bibliographical Note

Origami Birds is a new work, first published
by Dover Publications, Inc., in 2013.

Library of Congress Cataloging-in-Publication Data

Montroll, John.
 Origami birds / John Montroll.
    pages cm
 ISBN-13: 978-0-486-49827-0
 ISBN-10: 0-486-49827-1
 1. Origami. 2. Birds in art. I. Title.
 TT872.5.M657   2013
 736'.982–dc23   2013009204

Manufactured in the United States by Courier Corporation
49827101   2013
www.doverpublications.com

Introduction

Birds are colorful, graceful animals which are well suited as origami subjects. Here is a flock of 34 original origami birds of various shapes and complexities. You can fold a penguin with its baby, the chicken family, peacock, turkey, canary, and many more, each from a single square sheet of paper with no cutting. Throughout, you can learn techniques in forming wings, legs, tails, and beaks.

The birds are sorted alphabetically from anhinga to woodpecker. Priority is given to capture the bird's spirit, such as the outstretched wings of the crane, head and tail detail of the rooster, eyes of the owl and baby penguin, and the quail's plumes. The models are designed for detail without being too complex. Each model is accompanied with a photo and information about the bird.

This book is part of a volume to simplify the organization of other books. Many models are new, and several were in older books which include *African Animals in Origami* and *Bugs and Birds in Origami*.

The diagrams are drawn in the internationally approved Randlett-Yoshizawa style, which is easy to follow once you have learned the basic folds. You can use any kind of square paper for these models, but the best results can be achieved using standard origami paper, which is colored on one side and white on the other. In these diagrams, the shading represents the colored side. Large sheets are easier to use than small ones. Origami supplies can be found in arts and craft shops, or at Dover Publications online: www.doverpublications.com. You can also visit OrigamiUSA at www.origamiusa.org for origami supplies and other related information including an extensive list of local, national, and international origami groups.

Several students from Saint Anselm's Abbey School added life to this work with photography and text. I thank Yanktoro Udoumoh for photographing all the models. Many thanks to Ryan Dalbec, Joseph St. Pierre, Avery Gray, Henry Beh, C.J. Pizzano, Nino Suffoletta, Thomas Bui, Conrad Vecchione, Matias Orrego, and Charlie Paquette for writing about the birds. I thank my editor, Charley Montroll. I thank Robert J. Lang for helping with the computer. Much thanks, also, to Himanshu Agrawal for his continued help with many facets of this work.

John Montroll

www.johnmontroll.com

Contents

★ Simple
★★ Intermediate
★★★ Complex

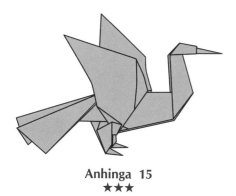

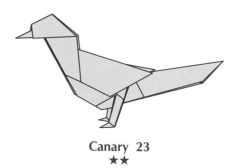

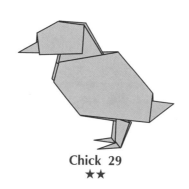

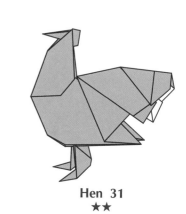

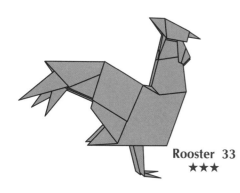

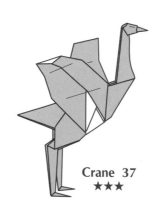

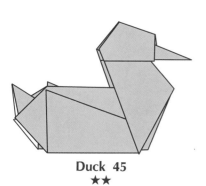

More ➡

Penguin 96
★★

Baby Penguin 99
★★★

Pigeon 103
★★

Quail 106
★★★

Roadrunner 110
★★

Stork 113
★★★

Swallow 118
★★

Swan 121
★★

Turkey 123
★★★

Woodpecker 127
★★

Symbols

Lines

— — — — — — — —   Valley fold, fold in front.

—··—··—··—··—··—   Mountain fold, fold behind.

————————   Crease line.

····························   X-ray or guide line.

Arrows

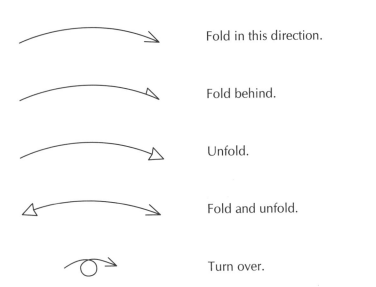

Fold in this direction.

Fold behind.

Unfold.

Fold and unfold.

Turn over.

Sink or three dimensional folding.

Place your finger between these layers.

Basic Folds

Pleat Fold.

Fold back and forth. Each pleat is composed of one valley and mountain fold. Here are two examples.

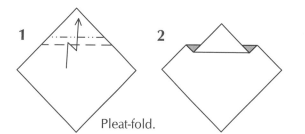

Pleat-fold.

Pleat-fold.

Squash Fold.

In a squash fold, some paper is opened and then made flat. The shaded arrow shows where to place your finger.

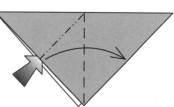
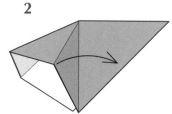
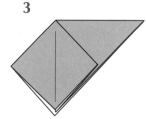

Squash-fold.

A 3D step.

Petal Fold.

In a petal fold, one point is folded up while two opposite sides meet each other.

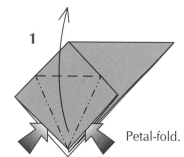
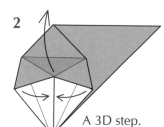
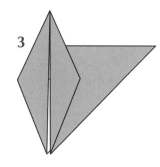

Petal-fold.

A 3D step.

Rabbit Ear.

To fold a rabbit ear, one corner is folded in half and laid down to a side.

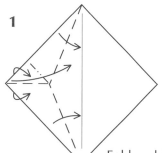
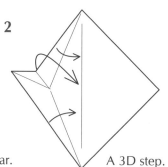

Fold a rabbit ear.

A 3D step.

Double Rabbit Ear.

If you were to bend a straw you would be folding the double rabbit ear.

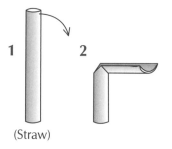
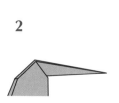

(Straw)

Double-rabbit-ear.

Inside Reverse Fold.

In an inside reverse fold, some paper is folded between layers. Here are two examples.

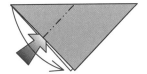

Reverse-fold.

Reverse-fold.

Outside Reverse Fold.

Much of the paper must be unfolded to make an outside reverse fold.

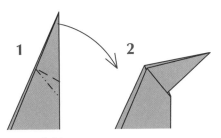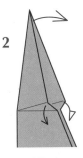

Outside-reverse-fold.

Crimp Fold.

A crimp fold is a combination of two reverse folds. Open the model slightly to form the crimp evenly on each side. Here are two examples.

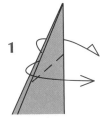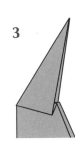

Crimp-fold.   Crimp-fold.   A 3D step.

Sink.

For a sink, some of the paper without edges is folded inside. To do this fold, much of the model must be unfolded.

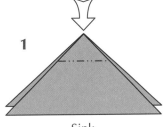

Sink.

Spread Squash Fold.

A cross between a squash fold and sink fold, some paper in the center is spread apart and then made flat.

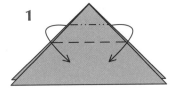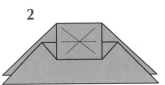

Spread-squash-fold.

Preliminary Fold.

The Preliminary Fold is the starting point for many models. The maneuver in step 3 occurs in many other models.

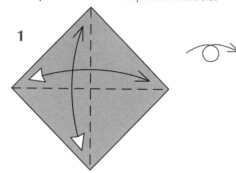

1

Fold and unfold.

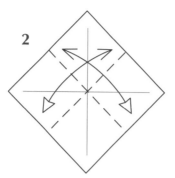

2

Fold and unfold.

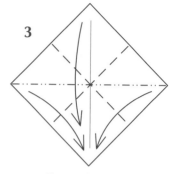

3

Collapse the square by bringing the four corners together.

4

This is 3D.

5

Preliminary Fold

Bird Base.

Historically, the Bird Base has been a very popular starting point. The folds used in it occur in many models.

1

Begin with the Preliminary Fold. Kite-fold, repeat behind.

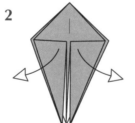

2

Unfold, repeat behind.

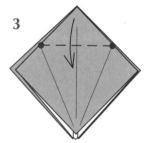

3

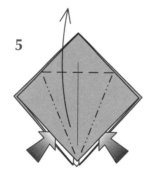

4

Unfold.

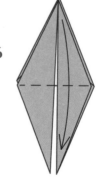

5

Petal-fold, repeat behind.

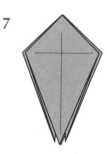

6

Repeat behind.

7

Bird Base

Blintz Frog Base.

This uses the double unwrap fold which is shown in detail below.

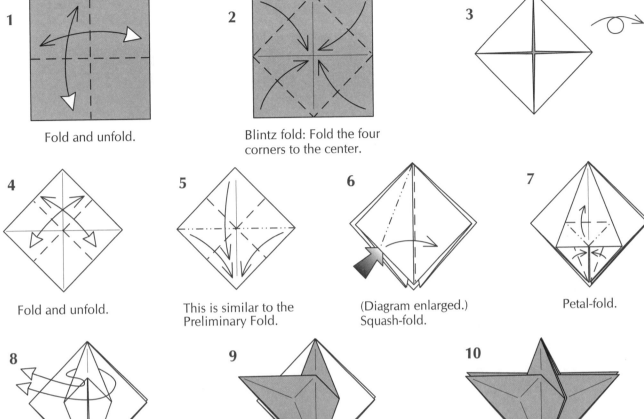

1

Fold and unfold.

2

Blintz fold: Fold the four corners to the center.

3

4

Fold and unfold.

5

This is similar to the Preliminary Fold.

6

(Diagram enlarged.) Squash-fold.

7

Petal-fold.

8

Double-unwrap-fold.

9

Repeat steps 6–8 three more times, on the back and sides.

10

Blintz Frog Base

Double Unwrap Fold.

In the double unwrap fold, locked layers are unwrapped and refolded. Much of the folding is 3D. The diagrams are depicted as shown in steps 8 and 9 of the Blintz Frog Base.

1

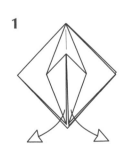

Begin with step 8 of the Blintz Frog Base. Spread at the bottom.

2

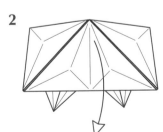

Unfold the top layer.

3

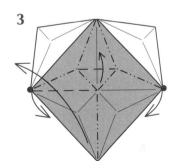

Refold along the creases. The dots will meet at the bottom.

4

Birds are incredible animals. They fill our world with beauty, wonder, and mystery. Throughout history, humans have been obsessed with the grace and bewitching charm of these small creatures. The ability to fly with such ease, precision, and speed has certainly inspired and challenged our world. Birds baffle us with their super capabilities including architectural and navigational skills. Science is still trying to understand how they perceive direction. Theories include mechanisms in the inner ear and the possibility that they "see" the magnetic field.

Flying and good vision go hand-in-hand, thus their vision is among the best of all animals. They have a wider viewing angle. They process images quicker than us. If we were to fly with them in a forest, the speed would blur our perception, but would remain clear to them. Many can see clearly at great distances, perhaps up to ten times sharper than us, including magnification at the center of their gaze. While our world of color is from three cones, many birds have four or more cones, spanning the ultraviolet spectrum. Their world is far more colorful, experiencing colors unimaginable. What they see as a beautiful flower with detailed patterns in the ultraviolet range is plain white to us.

These social animals, the progeny of dinosaurs, remarkably talented and varied, fill the world with their beauty and song. Their determination and stamina to make extremely long flights, spanning the globe, are an inspiration to us. These elegant creatures are a perfect testimony to evolution. We may emulate them with our machines, but the elegance and genius of birds remains unparalleled in our world.

Anhinga

The anhinga is found in warm, wet climates in the Americas. It is about 33 inches long with a wingspan of 46 inches and weighs about 3 lbs. It is also known as "Snake Bird" because it resembles the head of a snake when it is swimming in the water looking for food.

1

Fold and unfold.

2

Kite-fold and unfold.

3

Fold and unfold by the edge.

4

Fold and unfold by the diagonal.

5

6

Fold and unfold the top layer.

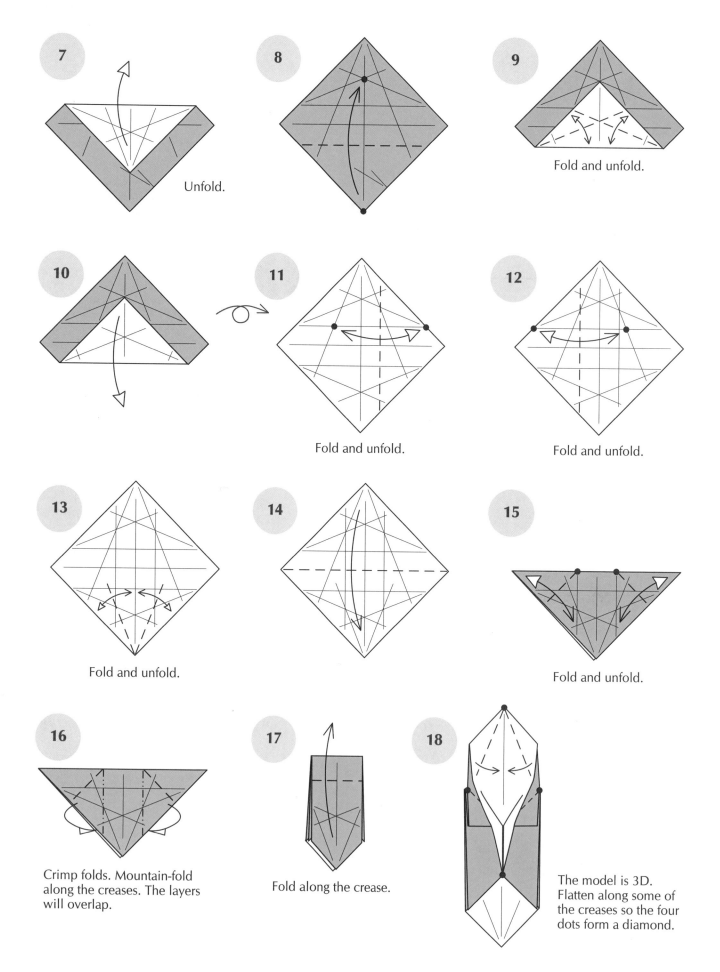

7 Unfold.

8 Fold and unfold.

9 Fold and unfold.

10

11 Fold and unfold.

12 Fold and unfold.

13 Fold and unfold.

14

15 Fold and unfold.

16 Crimp folds. Mountain-fold along the creases. The layers will overlap.

17 Fold along the crease.

18 The model is 3D. Flatten along some of the creases so the four dots form a diamond.

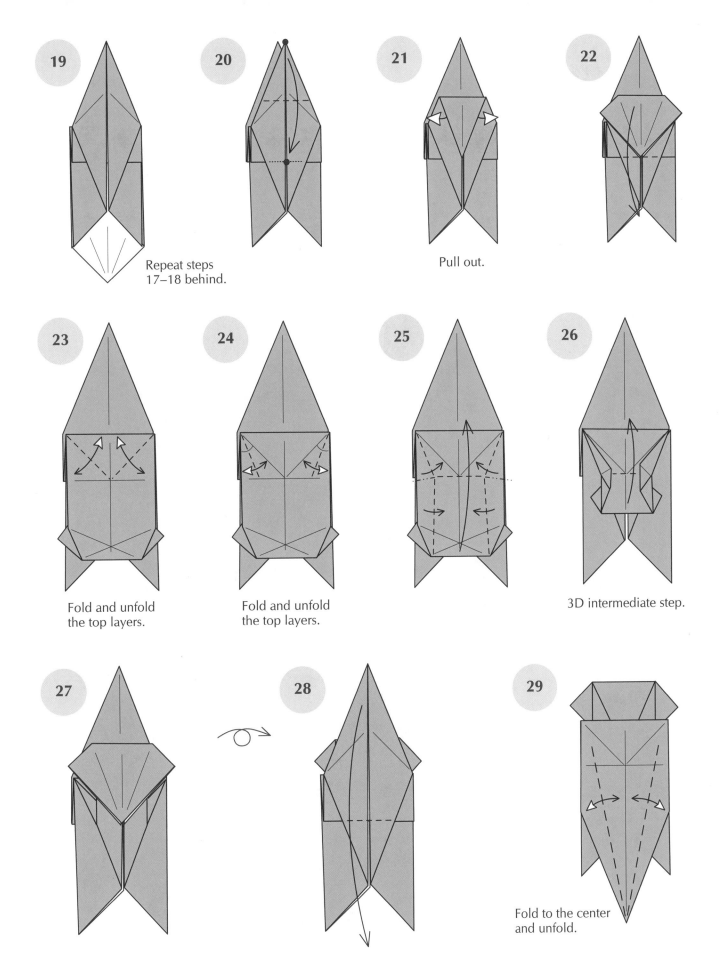

19 Repeat steps 17–18 behind.

20

21 Pull out.

22

23 Fold and unfold the top layers.

24 Fold and unfold the top layers.

25

26 3D intermediate step.

27

28

29 Fold to the center and unfold.

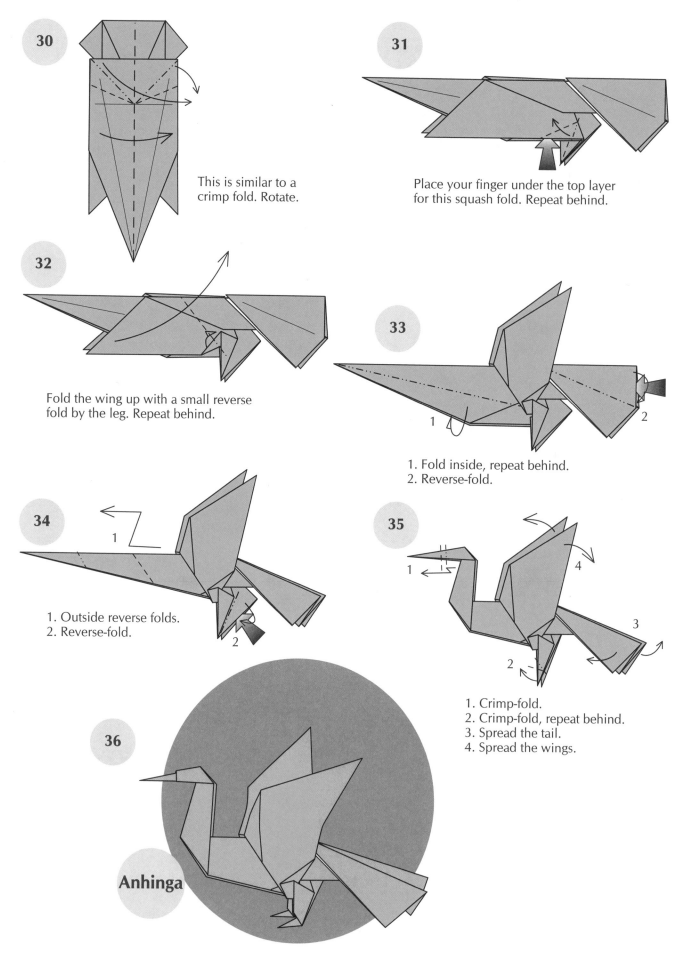

30

This is similar to a
crimp fold. Rotate.

31

Place your finger under the top layer
for this squash fold. Repeat behind.

32

Fold the wing up with a small reverse
fold by the leg. Repeat behind.

33

1. Fold inside, repeat behind.
2. Reverse-fold.

34

1. Outside reverse folds.
2. Reverse-fold.

35

1. Crimp-fold.
2. Crimp-fold, repeat behind.
3. Spread the tail.
4. Spread the wings.

36

Anhinga

Bee-eater

Bee-eaters are very colorful birds found in tropical and subtropical climates. Noted for their brilliant plumage, they have rather long bills that are slightly curved downward and sharply pointed. Bee-eaters range in length from 6 to 14 inches. Many bee-eaters have elongated central tail feathers. They feed primarily on bees, wasps, and other insects.

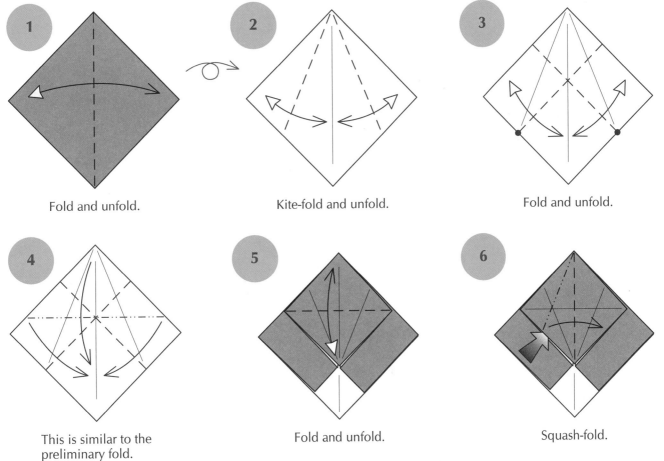

1 Fold and unfold.

2 Kite-fold and unfold.

3 Fold and unfold.

4 This is similar to the preliminary fold.

5 Fold and unfold.

6 Squash-fold.

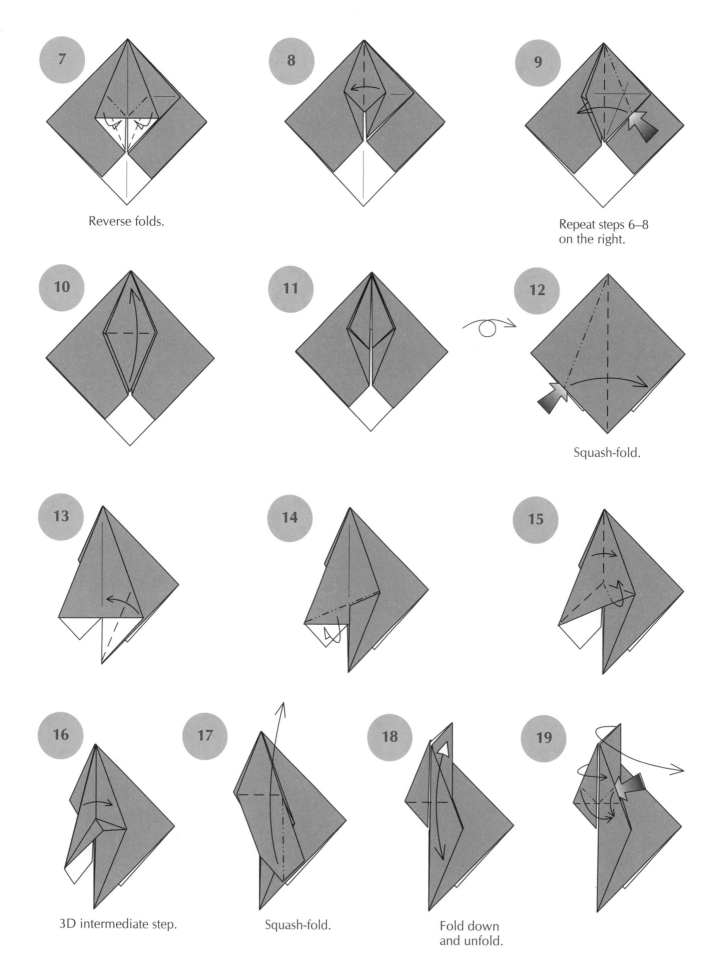

7 Reverse folds.

8

9 Repeat steps 6–8 on the right.

10

11

12 Squash-fold.

13

14

15

16 3D intermediate step.

17 Squash-fold.

18 Fold down and unfold.

19

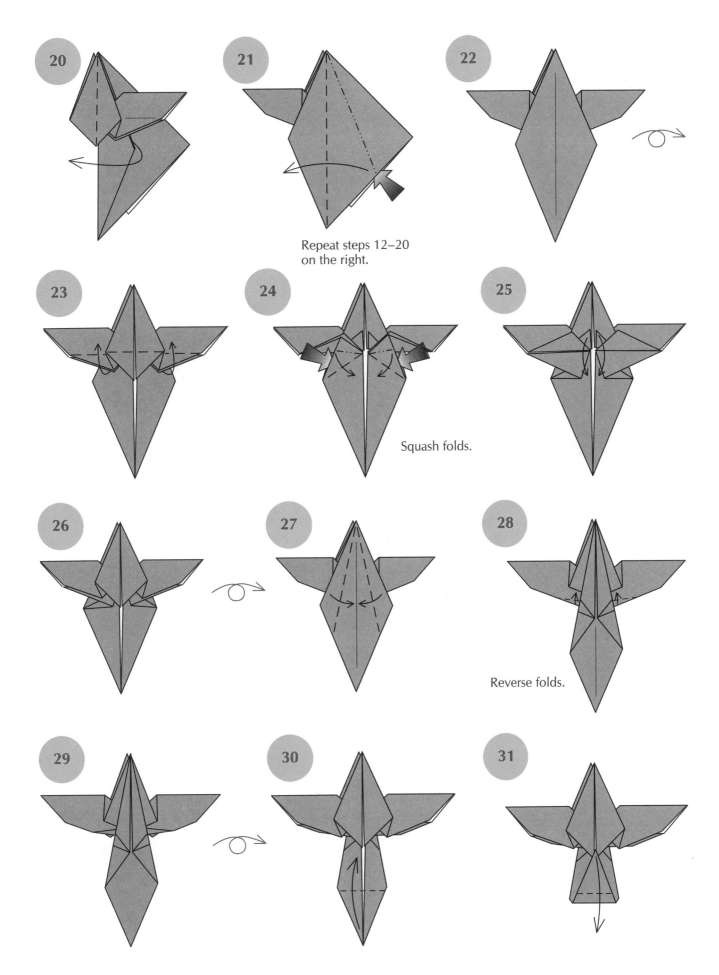

20

21

Repeat steps 12–20
on the right.

22

23

24

Squash folds.

25

26

27

28

Reverse folds.

29

30

31

32

Squash folds.

33

Place the darker paper above the lower part.

34

35

1. Rabbit-ear, repeat behind.
2. Outside-reverse-fold.

36

1
2
3

1. Outside-reverse-fold.
2. Fold behind.
3. Shape the tail.
Repeat behind.

37

1
2
3

1. Thin the beak.
2. Pleat the wings.
3. Fold the tail out.
Repeat behind.

38

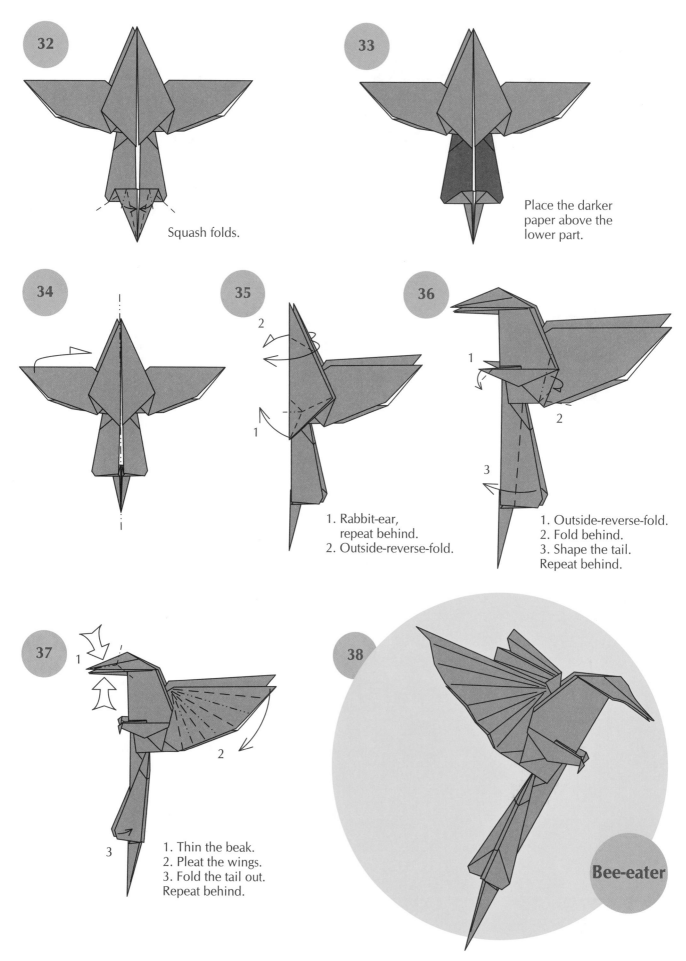

Bee-eater

Canary

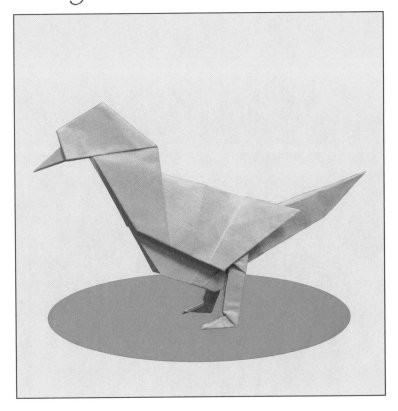

The Regular Canary is a domesticated canary species found on the islands off the coast of Morocco. Canaries became popular as house pets during the 17th century after being brought by Spanish sailors to Europe in limited demand to make them more expensive. Canaries are still popular today because of their singing voices.

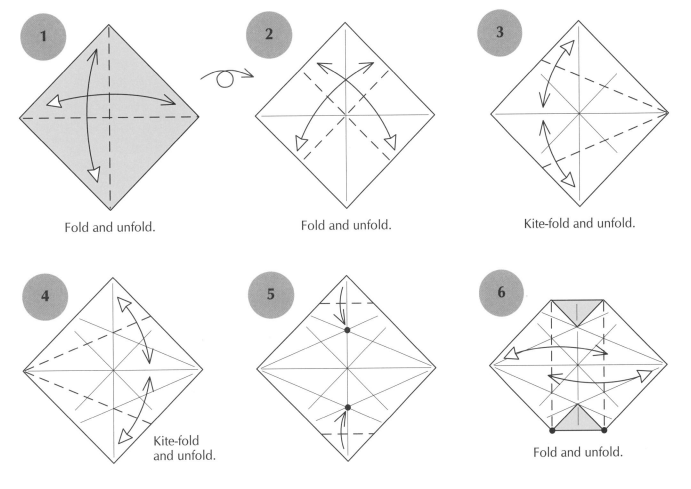

1 Fold and unfold.

2 Fold and unfold.

3 Kite-fold and unfold.

4 Kite-fold and unfold.

5

6 Fold and unfold.

7

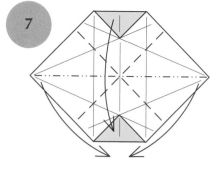

This is similar to the preliminary fold.

8

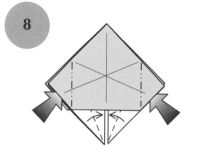

Reverse folds.
Repeat behind.

9

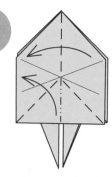

Repeat behind.

10

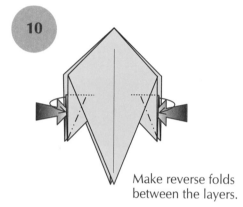

Make reverse folds between the layers.

11

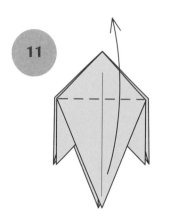

12

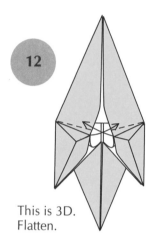

This is 3D.
Flatten.

13

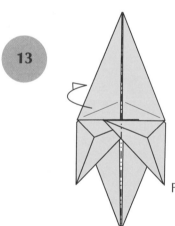

Fold in half and rotate.

14

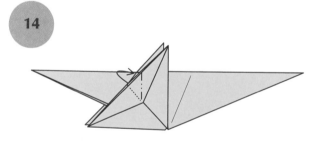

Reverse-fold between the layers and repeat behind.

15

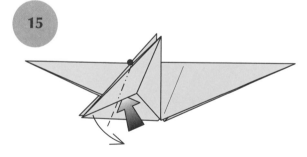

Reverse-fold and repeat behind.

16

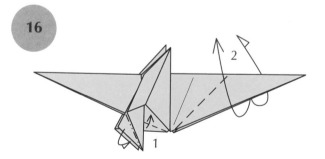

1. Repeat behind.
2. Outside-reverse-fold along the hidden edge.

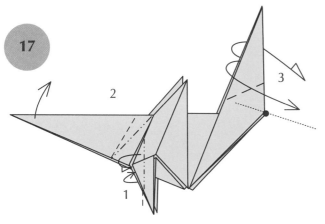

17

1. Fold both layers inside, repeat behind.
2. Crimp-fold.
3. Outside-reverse-fold so the edge meets the dot.

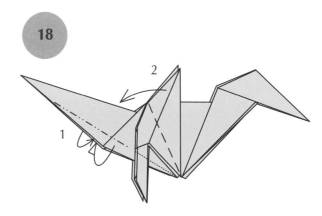

18

1. Fold inside.
2. Fold down.
Repeat behind.

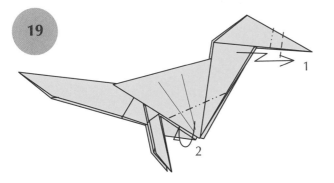

19

1. Crimp-fold.
2. Fold inside,
   repeat behind.

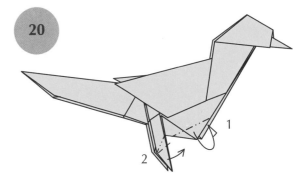

20

1. Fold inside.
2. Crimp-fold.
Repeat behind.

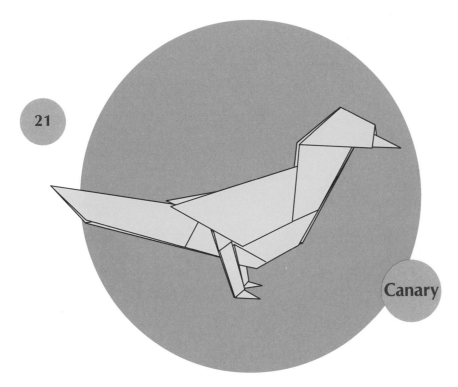

21

Canary

Cardinal

The cardinal, with its distinguishing crest, is an aggressive and territorial bird. It lives in woodlands, thickets, parks, and gardens. The male cardinal is bright red and the female is brown with a little red on the wings, crest, and bill. With its strong bill, the cardinal can eat hard seeds, along with berries.

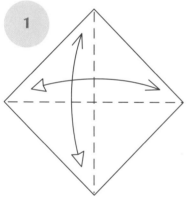

1

Fold and unfold.

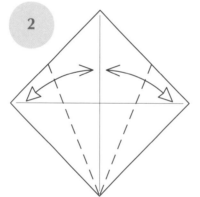

2

Kite-fold and unfold.

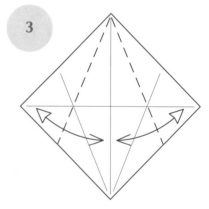

3

Kite-fold and unfold.

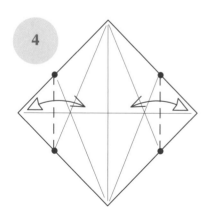

4

Fold and unfold.

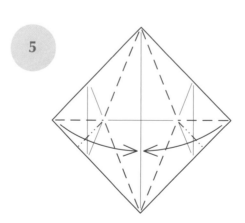

5

Rabbit ears.

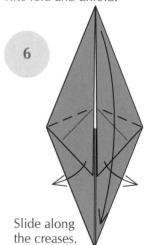

6

Slide along the creases.

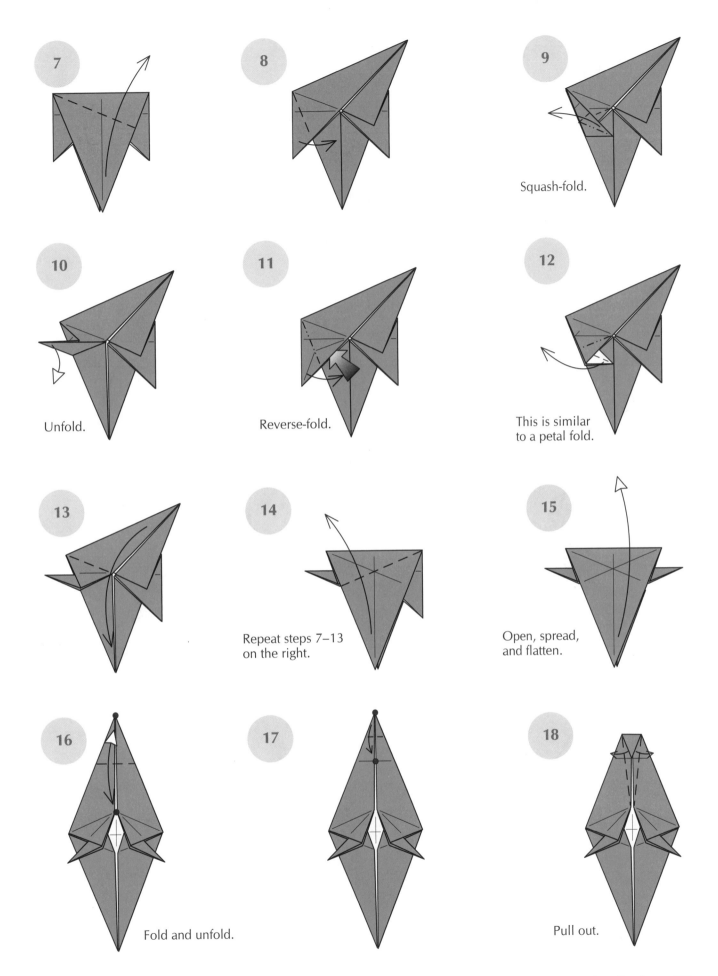

7

8

9

Squash-fold.

10

Unfold.

11

Reverse-fold.

12

This is similar
to a petal fold.

13

14

Repeat steps 7–13
on the right.

15

Open, spread,
and flatten.

16

Fold and unfold.

17

18

Pull out.

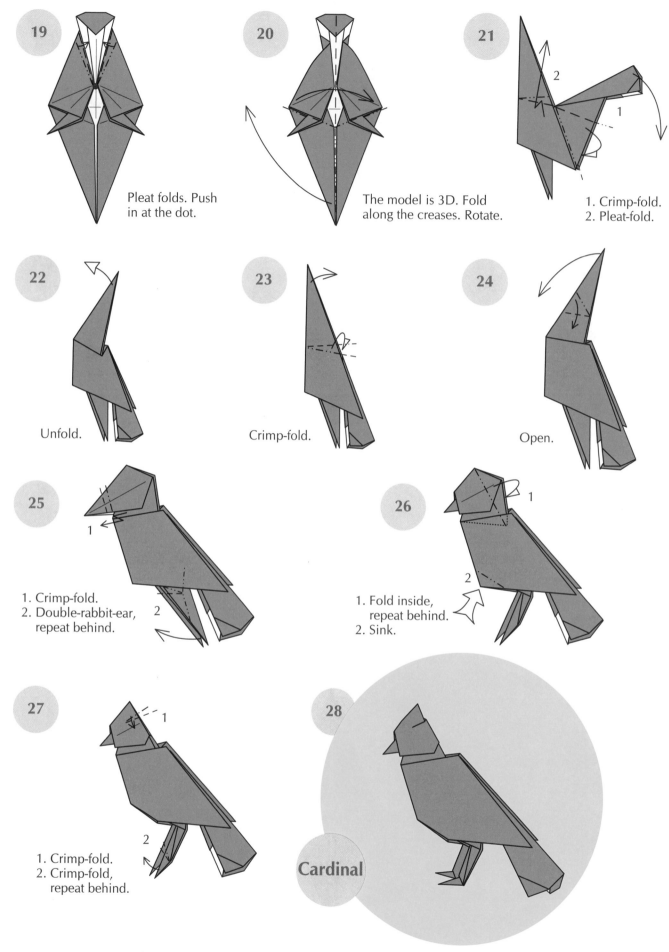

19

Pleat folds. Push in at the dot.

20

The model is 3D. Fold along the creases. Rotate.

21

1. Crimp-fold.
2. Pleat-fold.

22

Unfold.

23

Crimp-fold.

24

Open.

25

1. Crimp-fold.
2. Double-rabbit-ear, repeat behind.

26

1. Fold inside, repeat behind.
2. Sink.

27

1. Crimp-fold.
2. Crimp-fold, repeat behind.

28

Cardinal

Chick

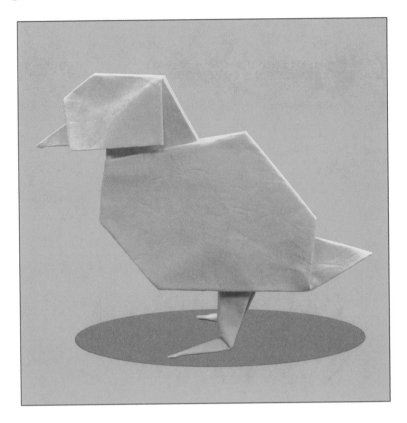

The chick is a baby chicken, and many people remember having egg incubators in the classroom when they were in Kindergarten or elementary school, and recall watching in amazement as the little chicks hatched from the eggs. The newly-hatched chicks are wet and tired from their exertions, but soon dry and become fluffy and begin their new lives.

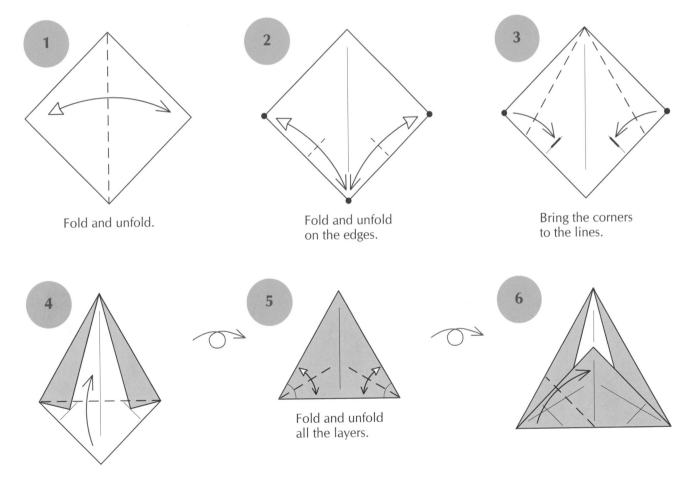

1 Fold and unfold.

2 Fold and unfold on the edges.

3 Bring the corners to the lines.

4

5 Fold and unfold all the layers.

6

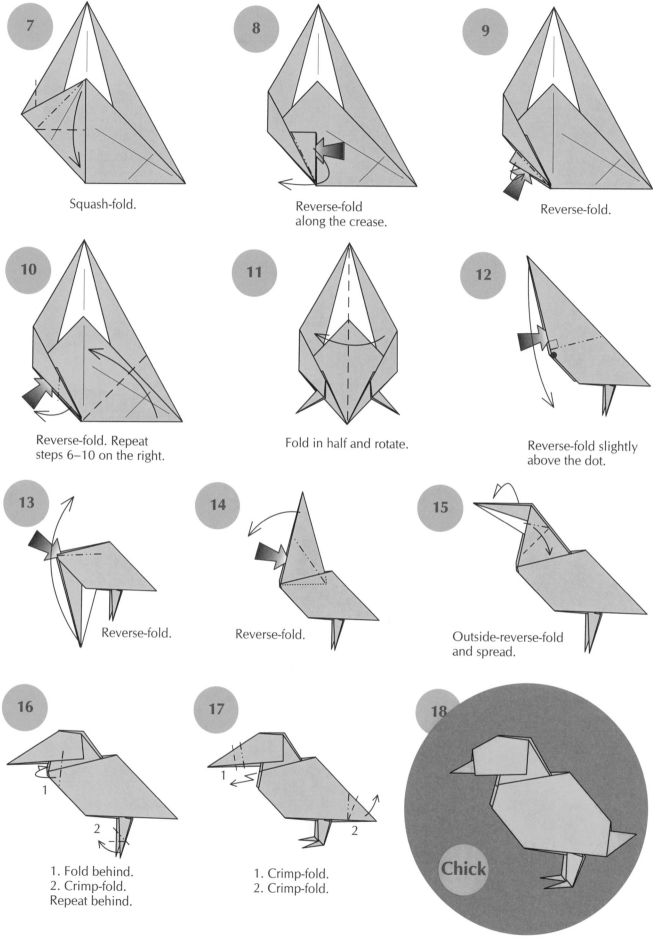

7 Squash-fold.

8 Reverse-fold along the crease.

9 Reverse-fold.

10 Reverse-fold. Repeat steps 6–10 on the right.

11 Fold in half and rotate.

12 Reverse-fold slightly above the dot.

13 Reverse-fold.

14 Reverse-fold.

15 Outside-reverse-fold and spread.

16
1. Fold behind.
2. Crimp-fold.
Repeat behind.

17
1. Crimp-fold.
2. Crimp-fold.

18 Chick

Hen

The domesticated hen had been part of human culture since ancient times as a provider of eggs and meat. Thought to have its origins on several continents at the same time, the hen, in terms of sheer numbers, has a living population in excess of 20 billion. Even in modern times, the hen makes a favored household pet, both on the farm and in suburban gardens.

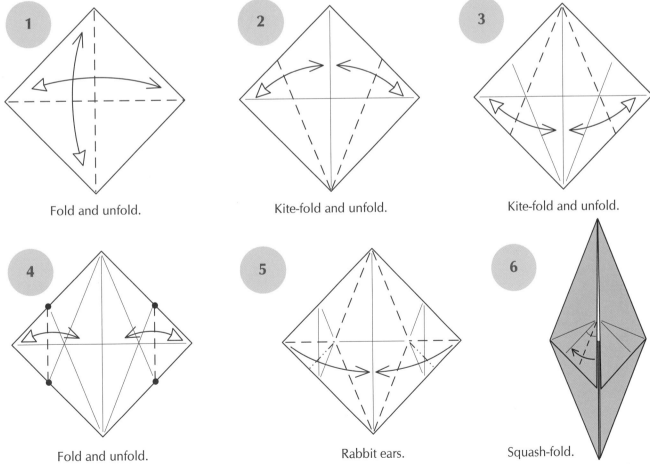

1 — Fold and unfold.

2 — Kite-fold and unfold.

3 — Kite-fold and unfold.

4 — Fold and unfold.

5 — Rabbit ears.

6 — Squash-fold.

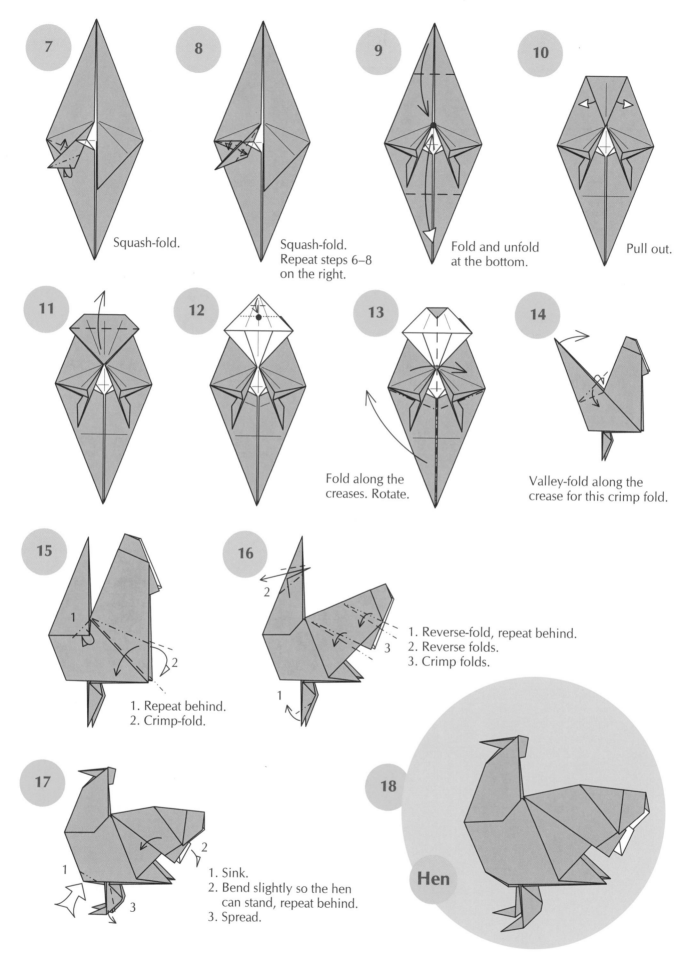

7 Squash-fold.

8 Squash-fold. Repeat steps 6–8 on the right.

9 Fold and unfold at the bottom.

10 Pull out.

11

12

13 Fold along the creases. Rotate.

14 Valley-fold along the crease for this crimp fold.

15 1. Repeat behind. 2. Crimp-fold.

16 1. Reverse-fold, repeat behind. 2. Reverse folds. 3. Crimp folds.

17 1. Sink. 2. Bend slightly so the hen can stand, repeat behind. 3. Spread.

18 Hen

Rooster

The rooster is a male chicken. The term originated from the United States, and is now widely used throughout the continent of North America as well as the countries of Australia and New Zealand. Though famous for crowing at the break of dawn, roosters will crow at almost any time of the day.

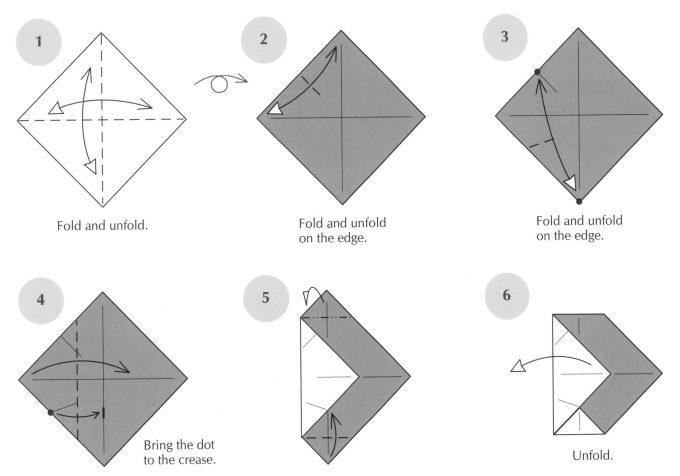

1

Fold and unfold.

2

Fold and unfold on the edge.

3

Fold and unfold on the edge.

4

Bring the dot to the crease.

5

6

Unfold.

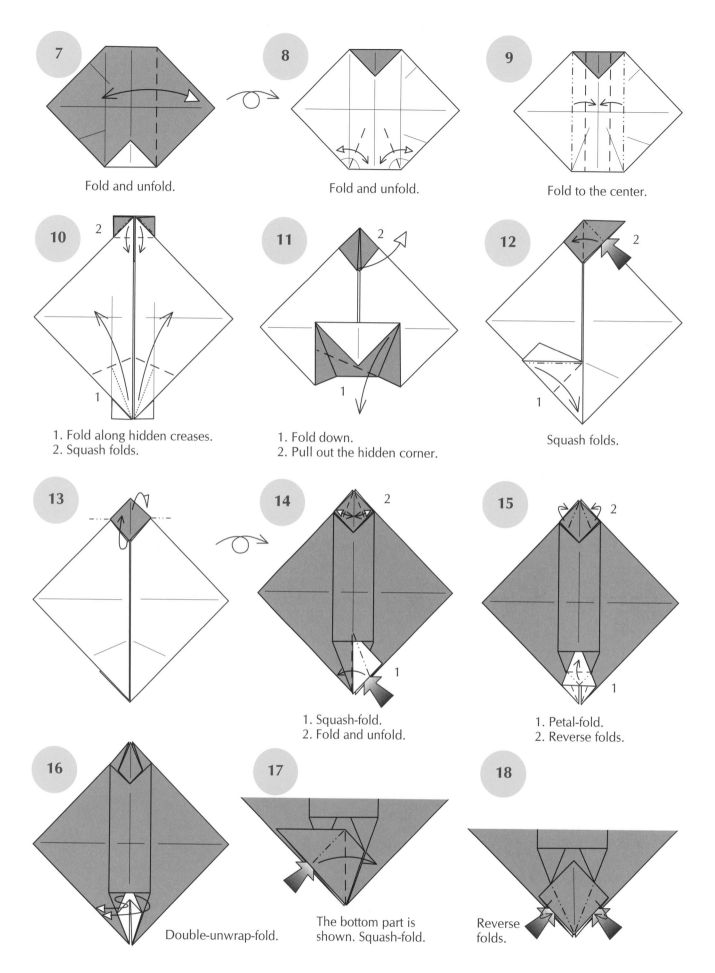

7 Fold and unfold.

8 Fold and unfold.

9 Fold to the center.

10
1. Fold along hidden creases.
2. Squash folds.

11
1. Fold down.
2. Pull out the hidden corner.

12 Squash folds.

13

14
1. Squash-fold.
2. Fold and unfold.

15
1. Petal-fold.
2. Reverse folds.

16 Double-unwrap-fold.

17 The bottom part is shown. Squash-fold.

18 Reverse folds.

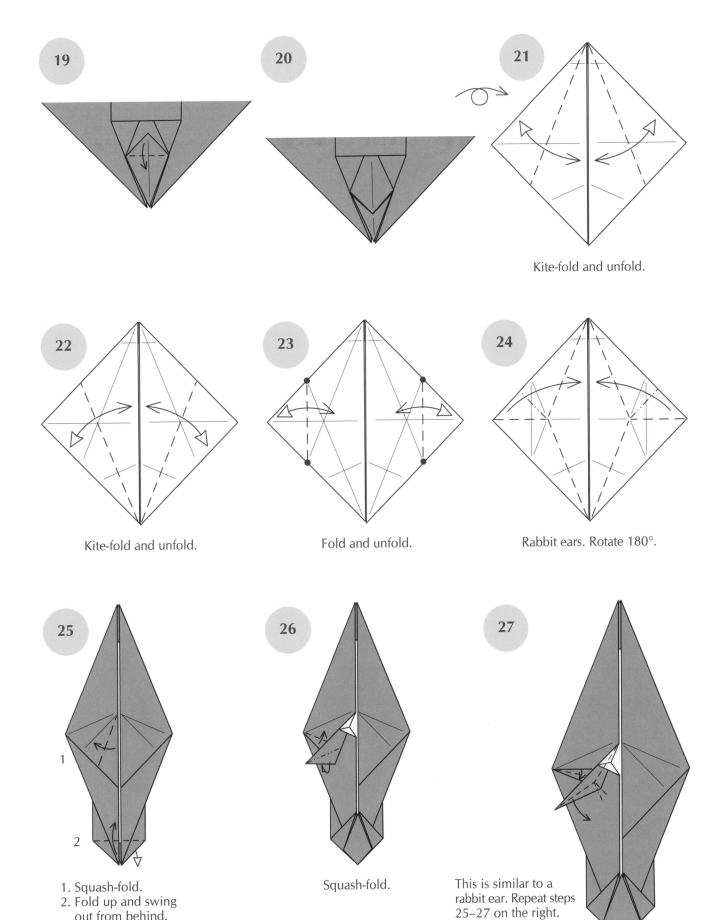

19

20

21

Kite-fold and unfold.

22

Kite-fold and unfold.

23

Fold and unfold.

24

Rabbit ears. Rotate 180°.

25

1. Squash-fold.
2. Fold up and swing out from behind.

26

Squash-fold.

27

This is similar to a rabbit ear. Repeat steps 25–27 on the right.

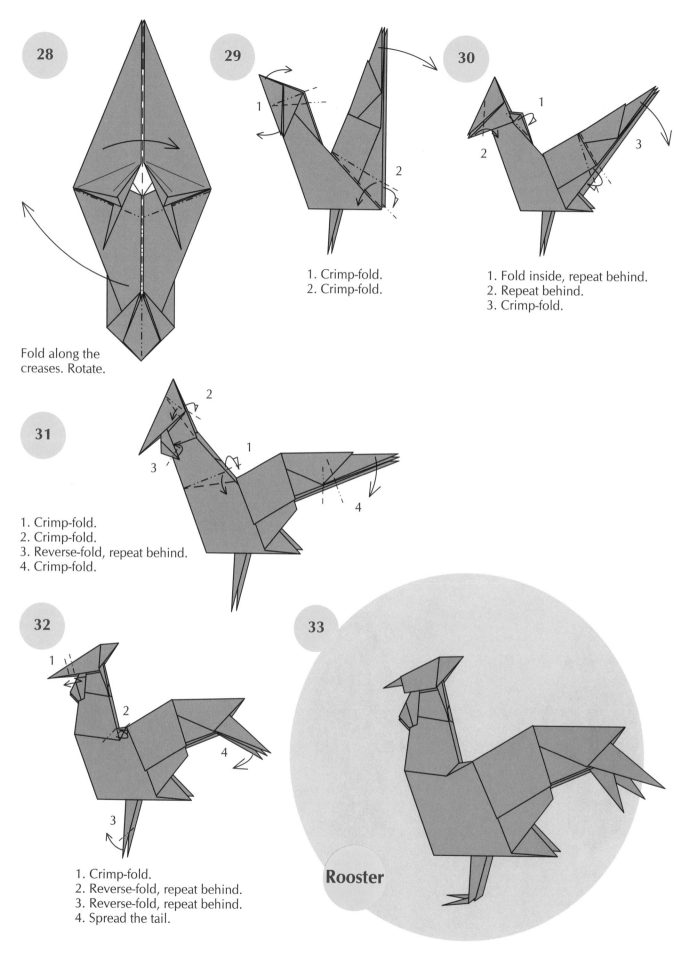

28

Fold along the
creases. Rotate.

29

1. Crimp-fold.
2. Crimp-fold.

30

1. Fold inside, repeat behind.
2. Repeat behind.
3. Crimp-fold.

31

1. Crimp-fold.
2. Crimp-fold.
3. Reverse-fold, repeat behind.
4. Crimp-fold.

32

1. Crimp-fold.
2. Reverse-fold, repeat behind.
3. Reverse-fold, repeat behind.
4. Spread the tail.

33

Rooster

Crane

Cranes are beautiful long-legged and long-necked birds. They often have decorative plumes on their heads. These social birds migrate in large flocks. Some species are rare and are bred in sanctuaries. Cranes have been incorporated into the myths and legends of many cultures, especially Asian cultures.

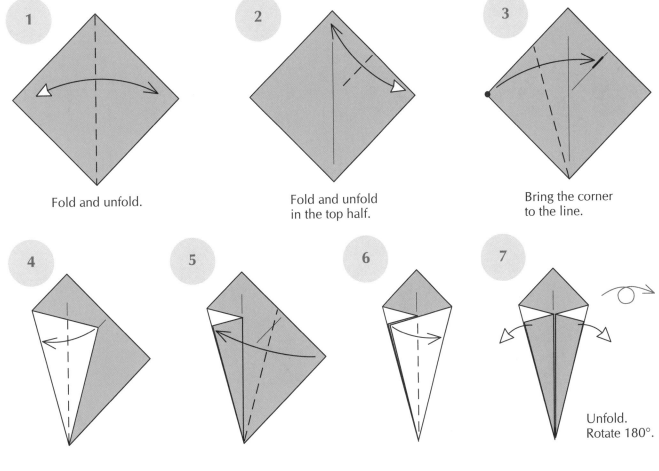

1

Fold and unfold.

2

Fold and unfold in the top half.

3

Bring the corner to the line.

4

5

6

7

Unfold.
Rotate 180°.

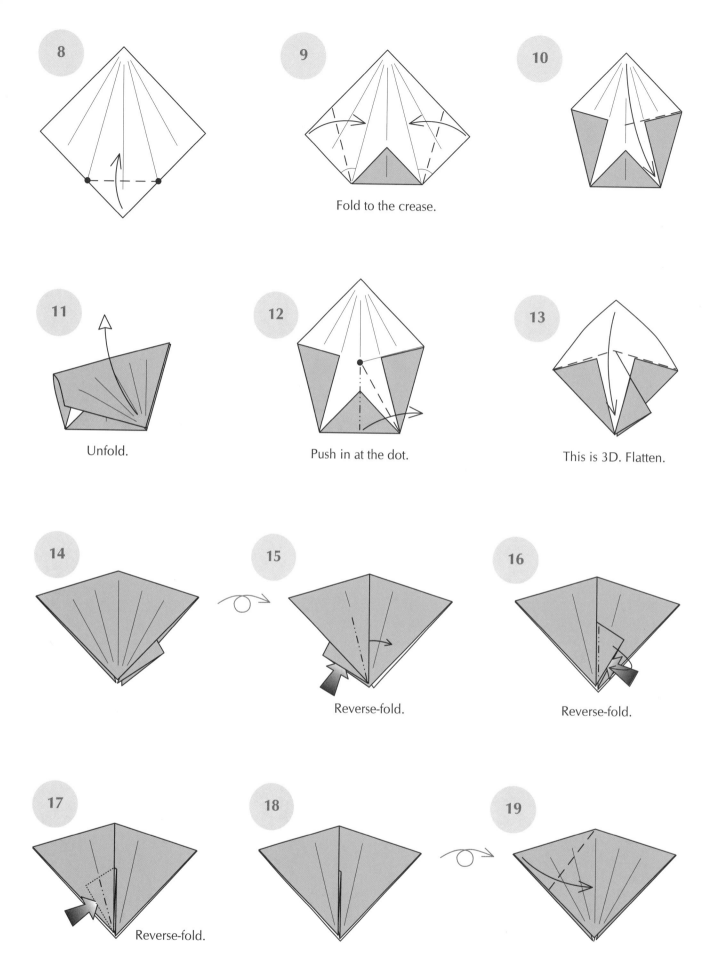

8

9

Fold to the crease.

10

11

Unfold.

12

Push in at the dot.

13

This is 3D. Flatten.

14

15

Reverse-fold.

16

Reverse-fold.

17

Reverse-fold.

18

19

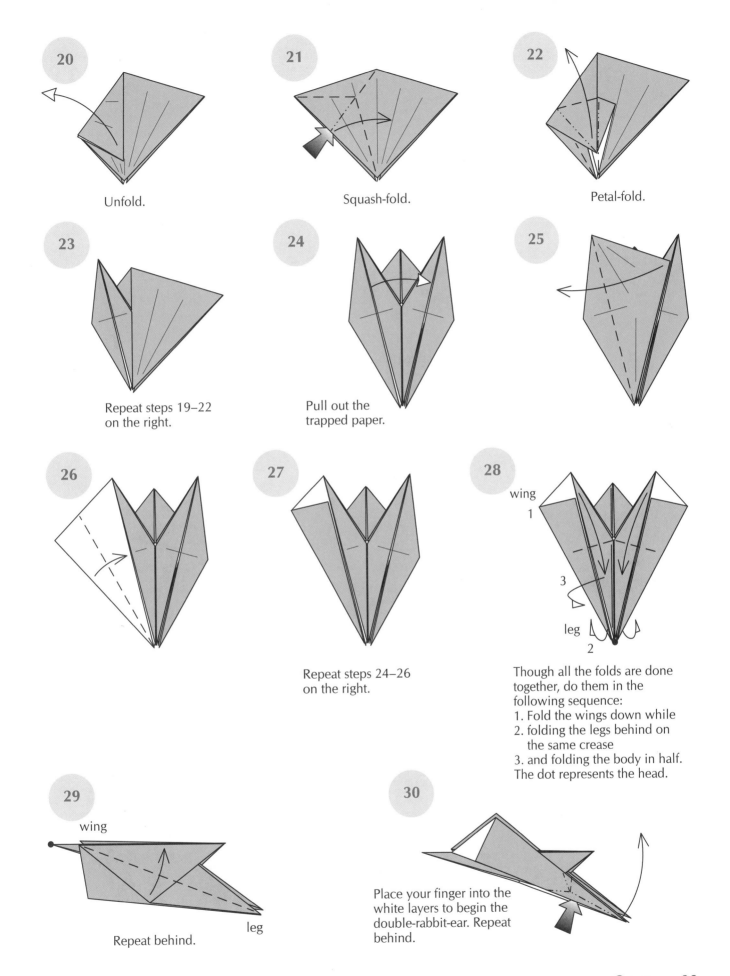

20 Unfold.

21 Squash-fold.

22 Petal-fold.

23 Repeat steps 19–22 on the right.

24 Pull out the trapped paper.

25

26

27 Repeat steps 24–26 on the right.

28 wing 1 3 leg 2

Though all the folds are done together, do them in the following sequence:
1. Fold the wings down while
2. folding the legs behind on the same crease
3. and folding the body in half. The dot represents the head.

29 wing leg

Repeat behind.

30 Place your finger into the white layers to begin the double-rabbit-ear. Repeat behind.

Crane 39

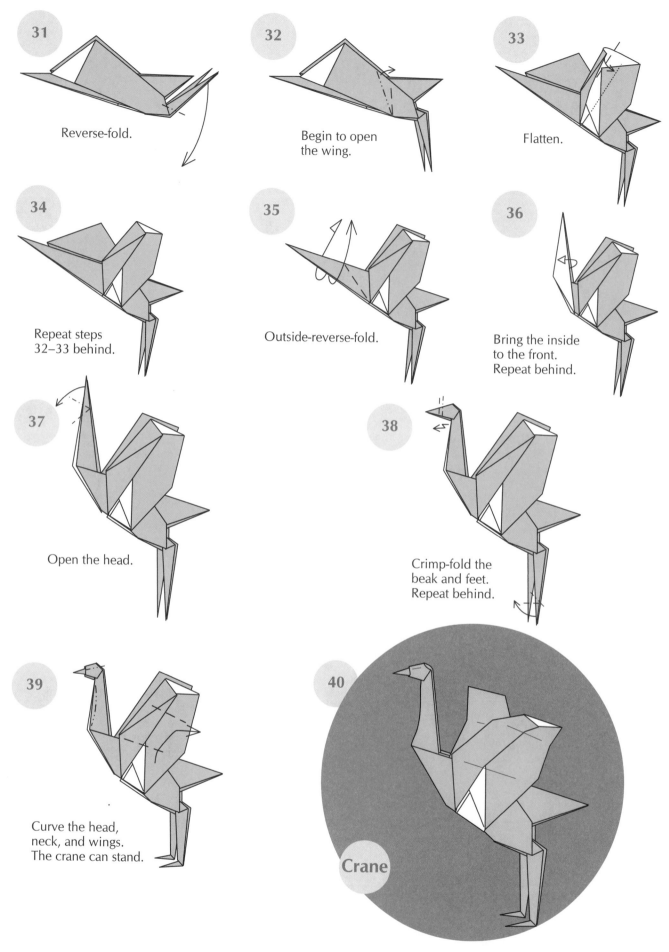

31 Reverse-fold.

32 Begin to open the wing.

33 Flatten.

34 Repeat steps 32–33 behind.

35 Outside-reverse-fold.

36 Bring the inside to the front. Repeat behind.

37 Open the head.

38 Crimp-fold the beak and feet. Repeat behind.

39 Curve the head, neck, and wings. The crane can stand.

40 Crane

Crowned Crane

Crowned cranes are colorful and named for the crown of straight, thin, white feathers on the back of their heads. They live in open landscapes and occasionally build their nests in trees. There are several sub-species. Black-necked cranes are popular in West Africa and are raised there as domestic animals. The grey-necked crane of South and Southeast Africa has a unique method of hunting for locusts; it stamps both feet repeatedly on the ground, scaring the insects and causing them to fly up. The crane can then devour them at its leisure.

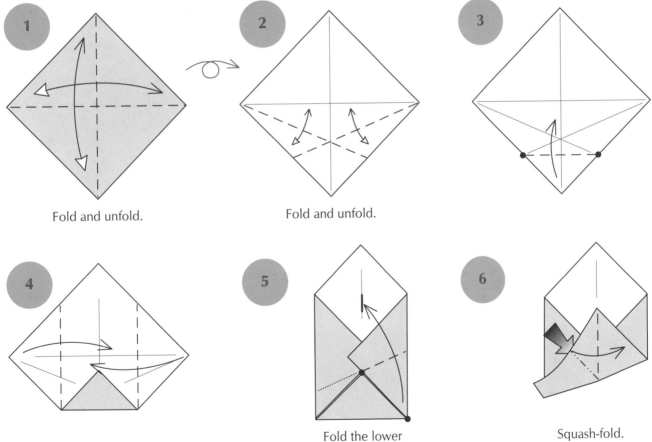

1 Fold and unfold.

2 Fold and unfold.

3

4

5 Fold the lower dot to the line.

6 Squash-fold.

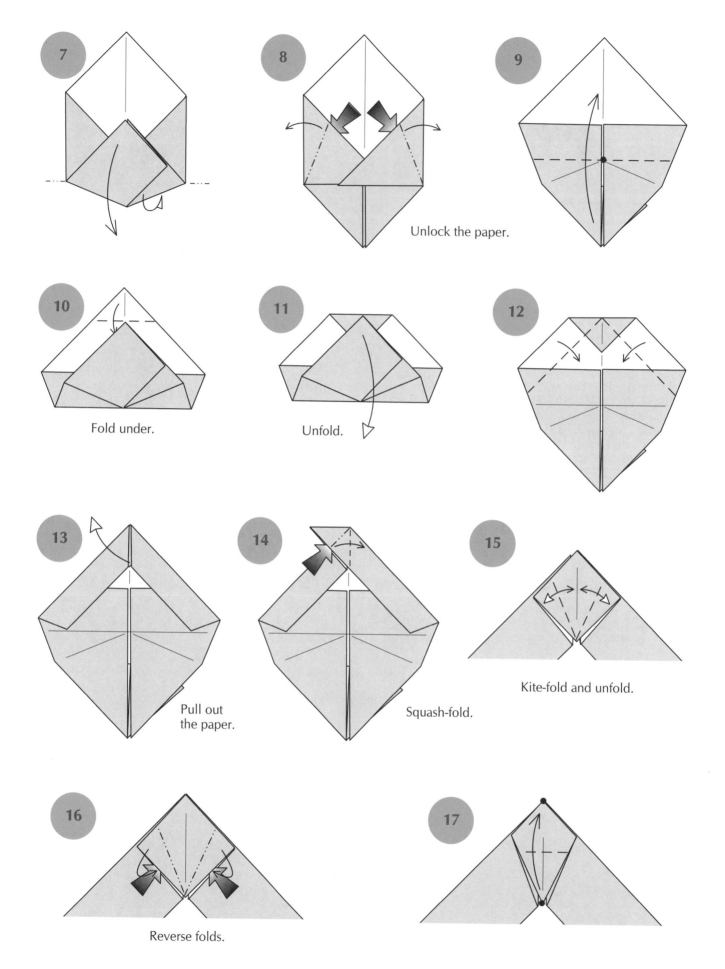

7

8

Unlock the paper.

9

10

Fold under.

11

Unfold.

12

13

Pull out
the paper.

14

Squash-fold.

15

Kite-fold and unfold.

16

Reverse folds.

17

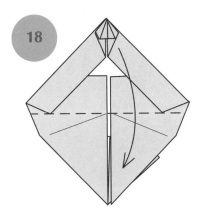

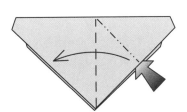

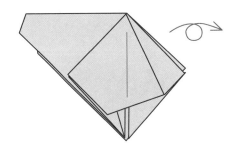

Squash-fold.

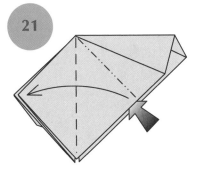

Squash-fold.

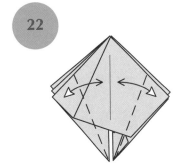

Kite-fold and unfold, repeat behind.

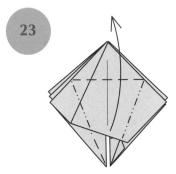

Petal-fold, repeat behind.

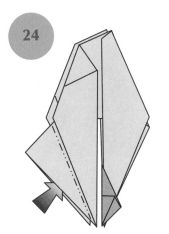

The darker paper used for the head is on the top layer. Reverse-fold.

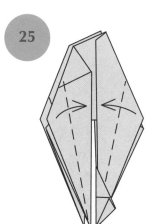

Repeat behind.

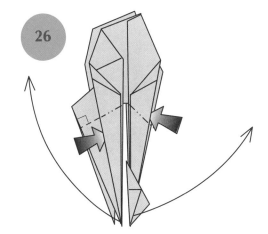

Reverse-fold the neck. Reverse-fold the legs at a right angle.

27

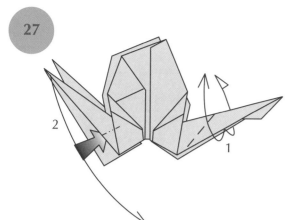

1. Outside-reverse-fold.
2. Reverse-fold, repeat behind.

28

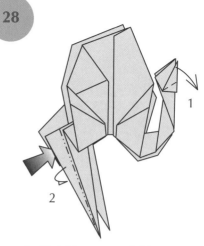

1. Outside-reverse-fold.
2. Thin the leg, repeat behind.

29

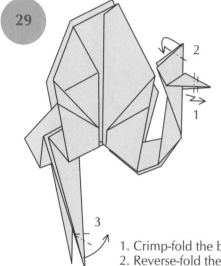

1. Crimp-fold the beak.
2. Reverse-fold the crown.
3. Spread the paper to form the foot, repeat behind.

30

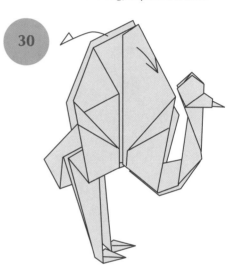

Spread the wings and puff out the body. Adjust the feet so the crane can stand.

31

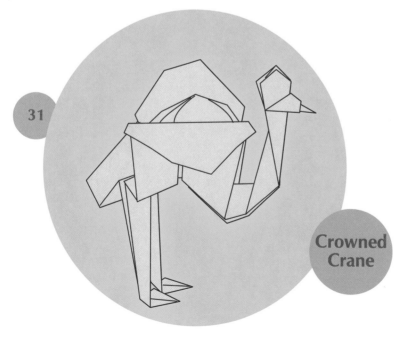

Crowned Crane

Duck

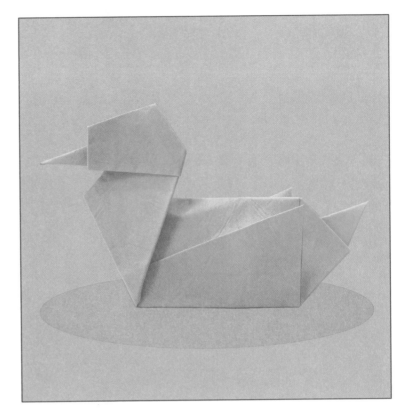

Ducks are mainly aquatic birds that can live in either salt water or fresh water. Swimming ducks feed by putting their head under water while their tails remain above. They feed on seeds, shoots, insects, mollusks, and worms.

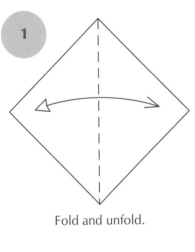

1

Fold and unfold.

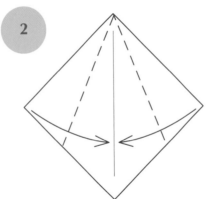

2

Kite-fold.

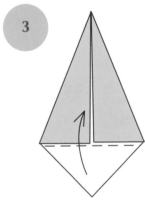

3

4

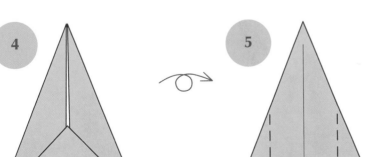

5

Fold to the center.

6

Unfold.

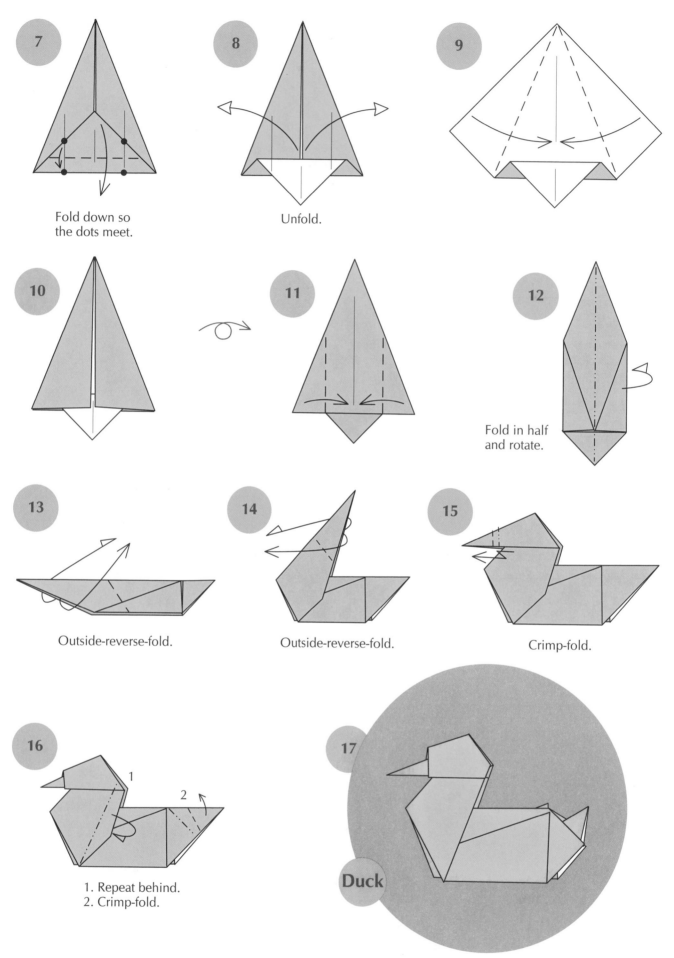

7

Fold down so
the dots meet.

8

Unfold.

9

10

11

12

Fold in half
and rotate.

13

Outside-reverse-fold.

14

Outside-reverse-fold.

15

Crimp-fold.

16

1
2

1. Repeat behind.
2. Crimp-fold.

17

Duck

Eagle

Eagles are large and powerful birds. They have large hooked beaks, powerful talons, and excellent eyesight. There are more than sixty species of these beautiful birds, and they usually construct their nests high up on a cliff or in a very high tree. Eagles represent strength, boldness, and daring and can often be seen on coats of arms and family crests.

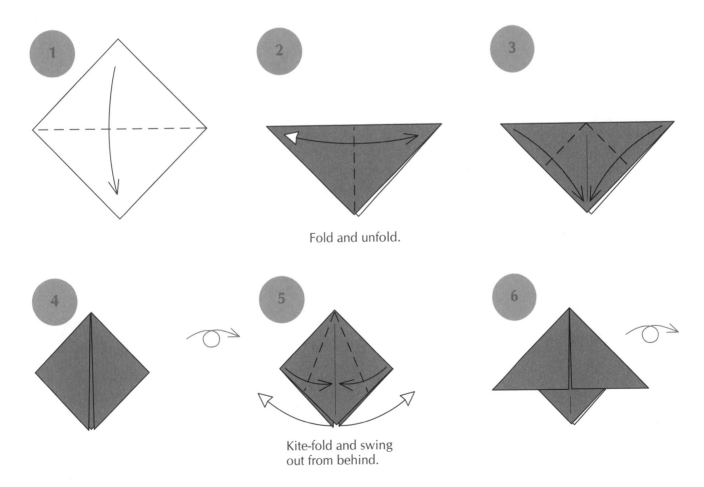

Fold and unfold.

Kite-fold and swing
out from behind.

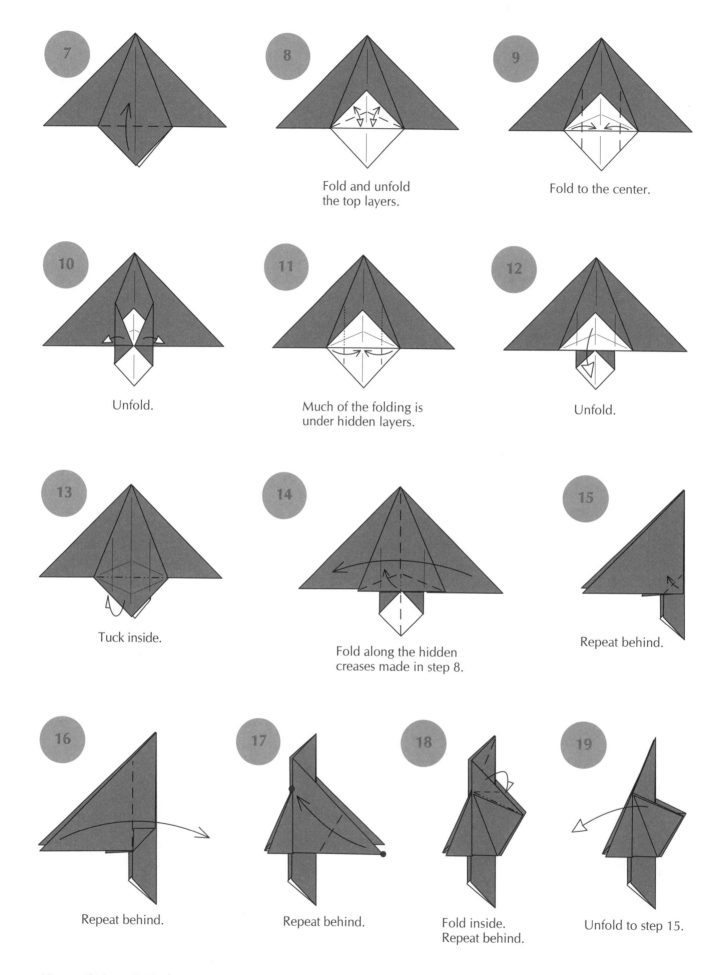

7

8
Fold and unfold
the top layers.

9
Fold to the center.

10
Unfold.

11
Much of the folding is
under hidden layers.

12
Unfold.

13
Tuck inside.

14
Fold along the hidden
creases made in step 8.

15
Repeat behind.

16
Repeat behind.

17
Repeat behind.

18
Fold inside.
Repeat behind.

19
Unfold to step 15.

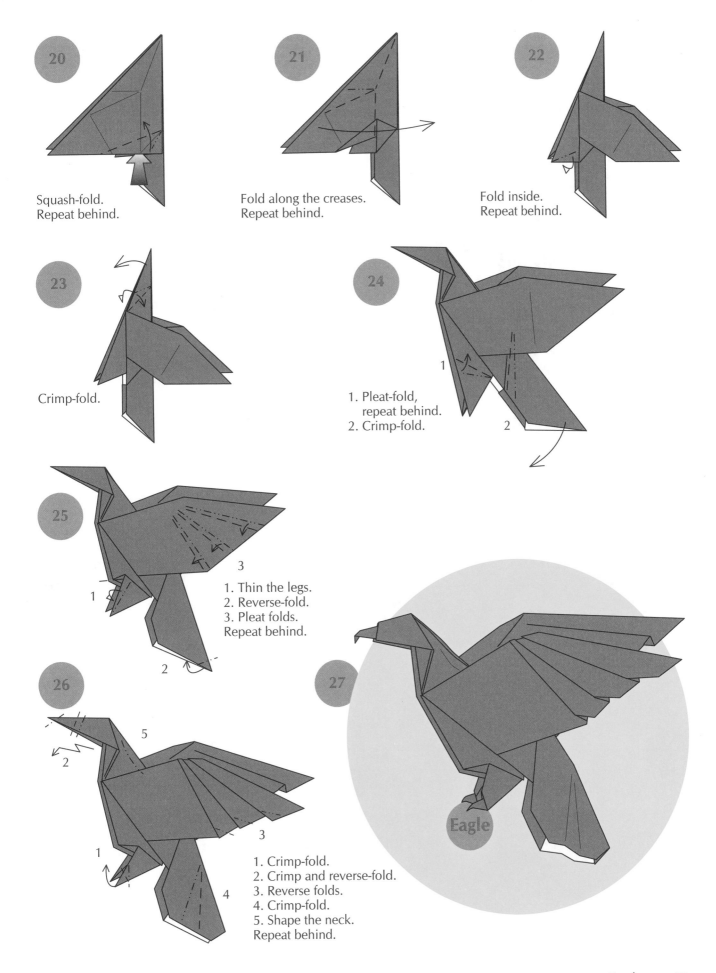

20 Squash-fold.
Repeat behind.

21 Fold along the creases.
Repeat behind.

22 Fold inside.
Repeat behind.

23 Crimp-fold.

24
1. Pleat-fold,
   repeat behind.
2. Crimp-fold.

25
1. Thin the legs.
2. Reverse-fold.
3. Pleat folds.
Repeat behind.

26
1. Crimp-fold.
2. Crimp and reverse-fold.
3. Reverse folds.
4. Crimp-fold.
5. Shape the neck.
Repeat behind.

27 Eagle

Eagle 49

Bald Eagle

The national bird of the United States of America, the bald eagle is one of the most elegant and majestic creatures in the wild. With wingspans of up to eight feet and sizes ranging from thirty to forty inches, bald eagles are birds which inspire respect in all other creatures. Found in both Canada and the United States, bald eagles use their strong talons to prey on fish, small animals, and, occasionally, other birds. They nest on the tops of trees and usually lay two eggs at a time. When bald eagles are young, they are completely brown; however, as they mature and grow, their head, neck, and tail feathers turn white.

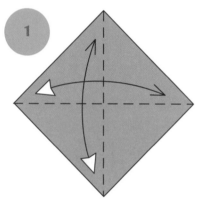

Fold and unfold.

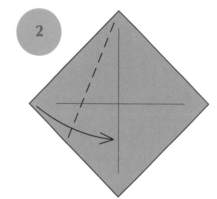

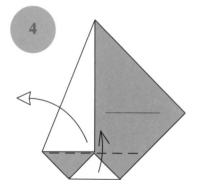

Fold the bottom up
and unfold on the left.

Fold and unfold.

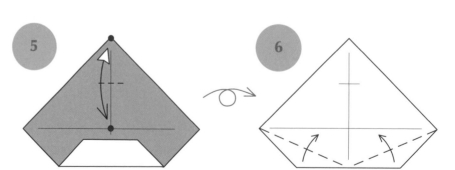

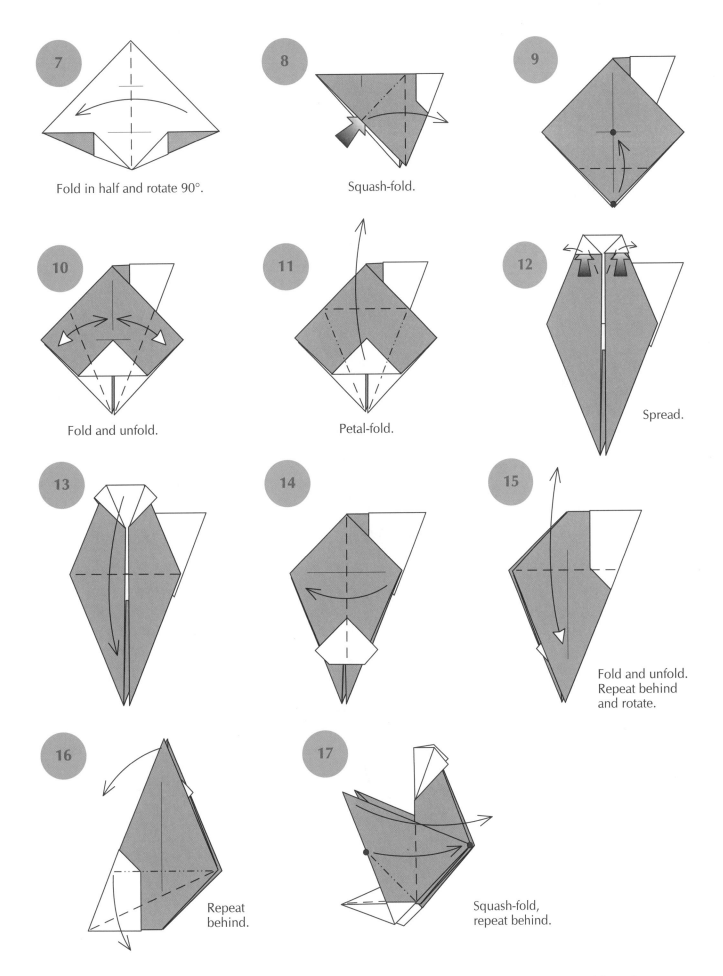

7

Fold in half and rotate 90°.

8

Squash-fold.

9

10

Fold and unfold.

11

Petal-fold.

12

Spread.

13

14

15

Fold and unfold.
Repeat behind
and rotate.

16

Repeat
behind.

17

Squash-fold,
repeat behind.

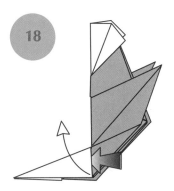

18

Pull out, repeat behind.

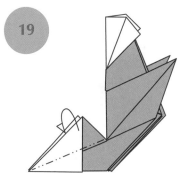

19

Fold into the center
layer, repeat behind.

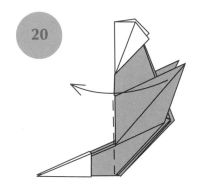

20

Repeat behind.

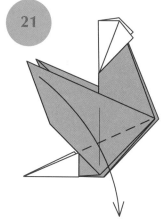

21

Repeat behind.

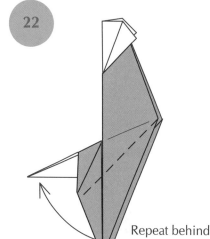

22

Repeat behind.

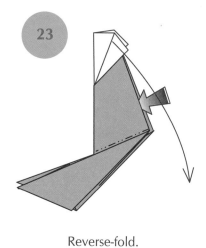

23

Reverse-fold.

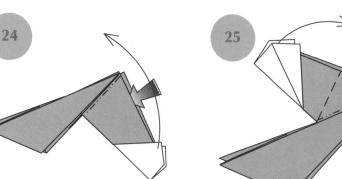

24

Reverse-fold.

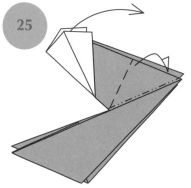

25

Crimp-fold.

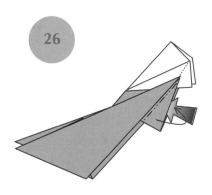

26

Reverse-fold,
repeat behind.

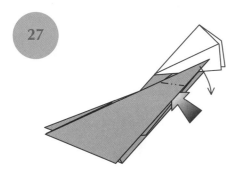

27

Reverse-fold, repeat behind.

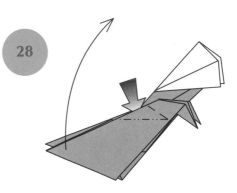

28

Squash-fold, repeat behind. Rotate.

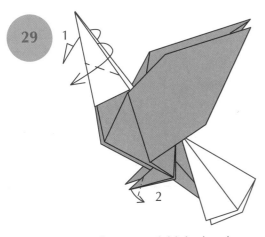

29

1. Outside-reverse-fold the head.
2. Reverse-fold the feet, repeat behind.

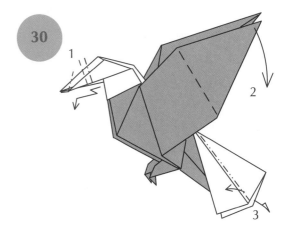

30

1. Shape the head with reverse folds.
2. Shape the wings.
3. Shape the tail.
Repeat behind.

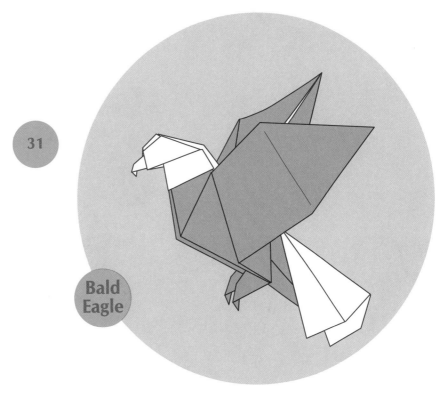

31

Bald Eagle

Flamingo

Flamingos are bright pink birds that are found in tropical climates and are known for their unusual behavior of standing on one leg. Their pink color comes from the bacteria that live in their main food sources, which are brine shrimp and blue-green algae, and malnourished flamingos are known to turn pale or white because of lack of food. They generally live in colonies that number in the thousands, and they mate for life.

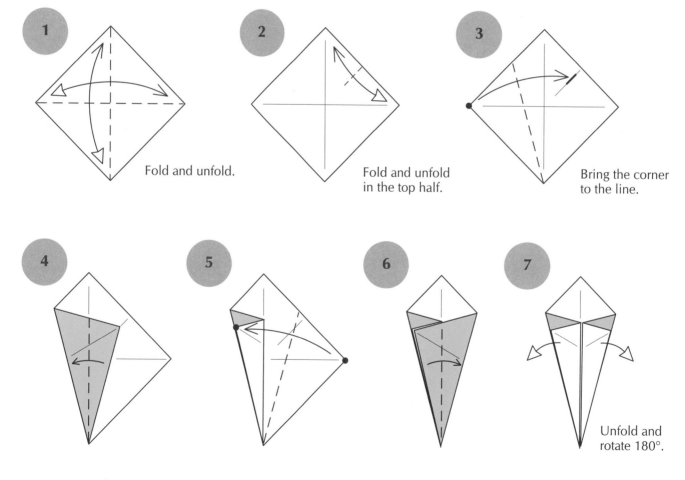

1 Fold and unfold.

2 Fold and unfold in the top half.

3 Bring the corner to the line.

4

5

6

7 Unfold and rotate 180°.

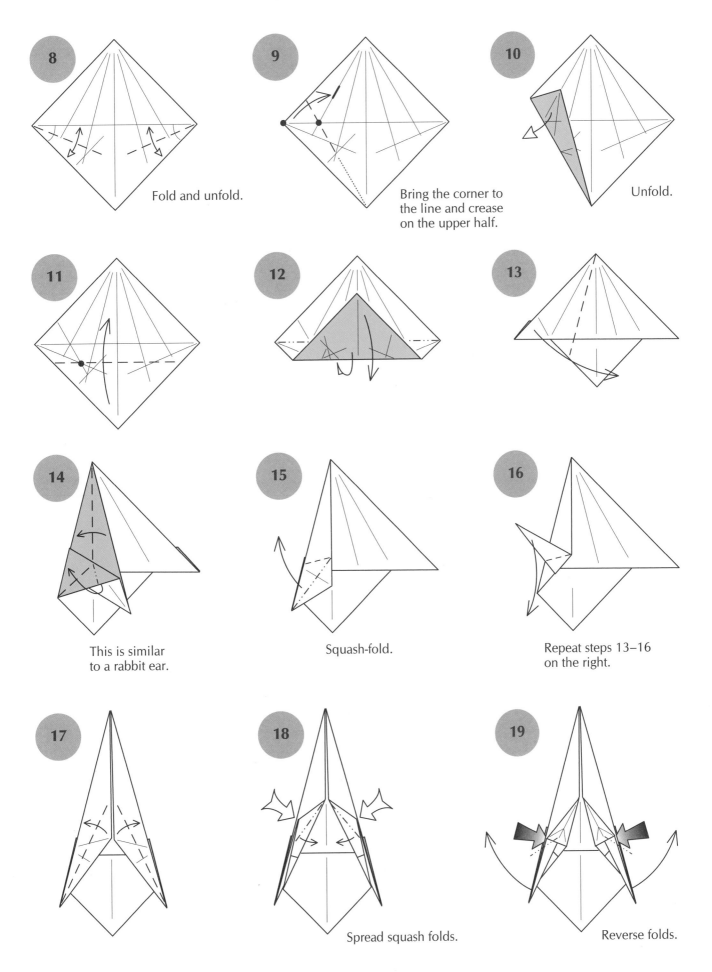

8 Fold and unfold.

9 Bring the corner to the line and crease on the upper half.

10 Unfold.

11

12

13

14 This is similar to a rabbit ear.

15 Squash-fold.

16 Repeat steps 13–16 on the right.

17

18 Spread squash folds.

19 Reverse folds.

Flamingo   55

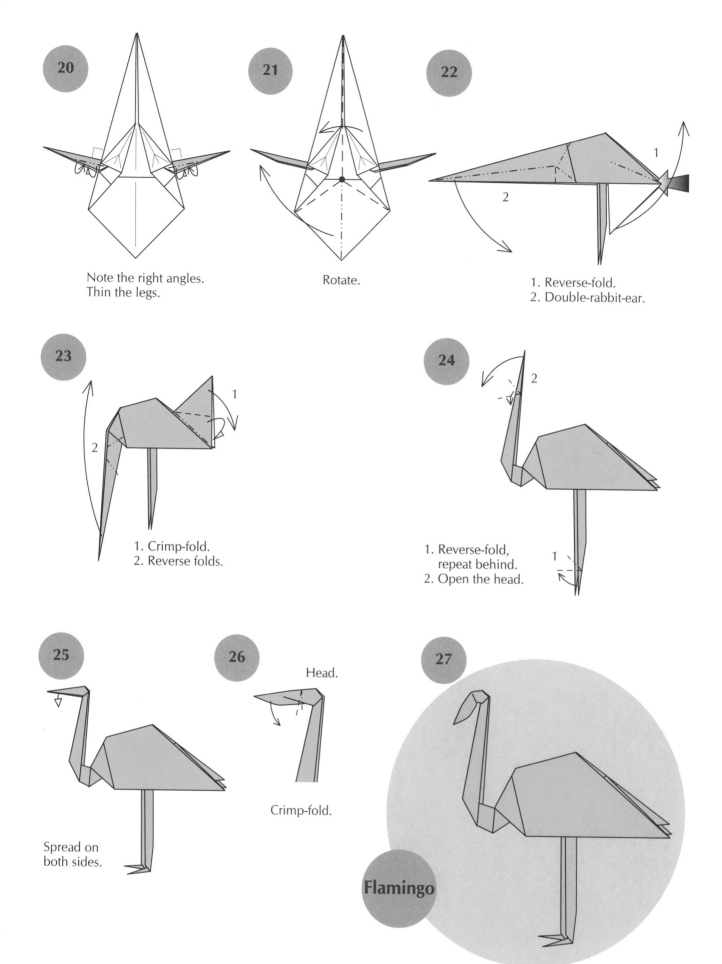

20

Note the right angles.
Thin the legs.

21

Rotate.

22

1
2

1. Reverse-fold.
2. Double-rabbit-ear.

23

1
2

1. Crimp-fold.
2. Reverse folds.

24

2

1

1. Reverse-fold,
   repeat behind.
2. Open the head.

25

Spread on
both sides.

26

Head.

Crimp-fold.

27

Flamingo

Goose

Geese are large wild or domestic waterfowl with long necks. They gather in large flocks feeding on grasses, seeds, and aquatic plants in grassy marshes and grain fields. Geese can be quite noisy, and they build nests on the ground from piles of grasses, roots, and sticks.

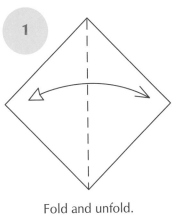

1

Fold and unfold.

2

Fold and unfold on the edges.

3

Bring the corners to the lines.

4

Fold and unfold.

5

6

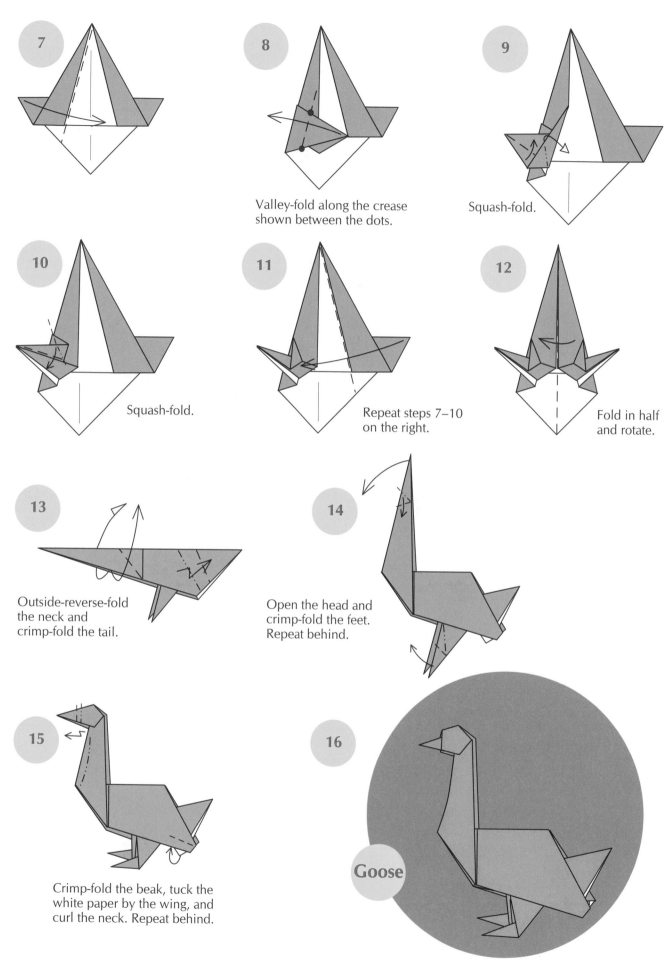

7

8

Valley-fold along the crease shown between the dots.

9

Squash-fold.

10

Squash-fold.

11

Repeat steps 7–10 on the right.

12

Fold in half and rotate.

13

Outside-reverse-fold the neck and crimp-fold the tail.

14

Open the head and crimp-fold the feet. Repeat behind.

15

Crimp-fold the beak, tuck the white paper by the wing, and curl the neck. Repeat behind.

16

Goose

Heron

Herons are birds which have long, slender necks, pointed bills, and large wings. The colors of a heron's plumage differ amongst species. Herons also come in many different sizes: some are as small as eighteen inches, while some are as large as forty-eight inches. Herons usually live near marshes or swamps, and they eat fish and almost any other animal life. The life span of a heron is between eleven to fifteen years. They sustain a relatively large population since most herons lay four to six eggs every year.

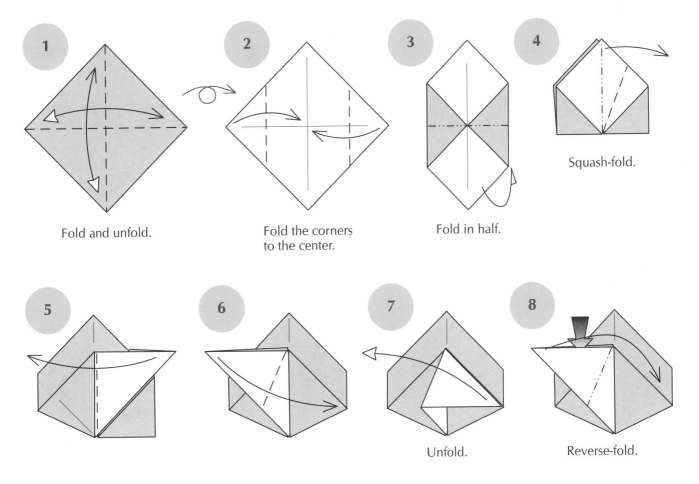

1 Fold and unfold.

2 Fold the corners to the center.

3 Fold in half.

4 Squash-fold.

5

6

7 Unfold.

8 Reverse-fold.

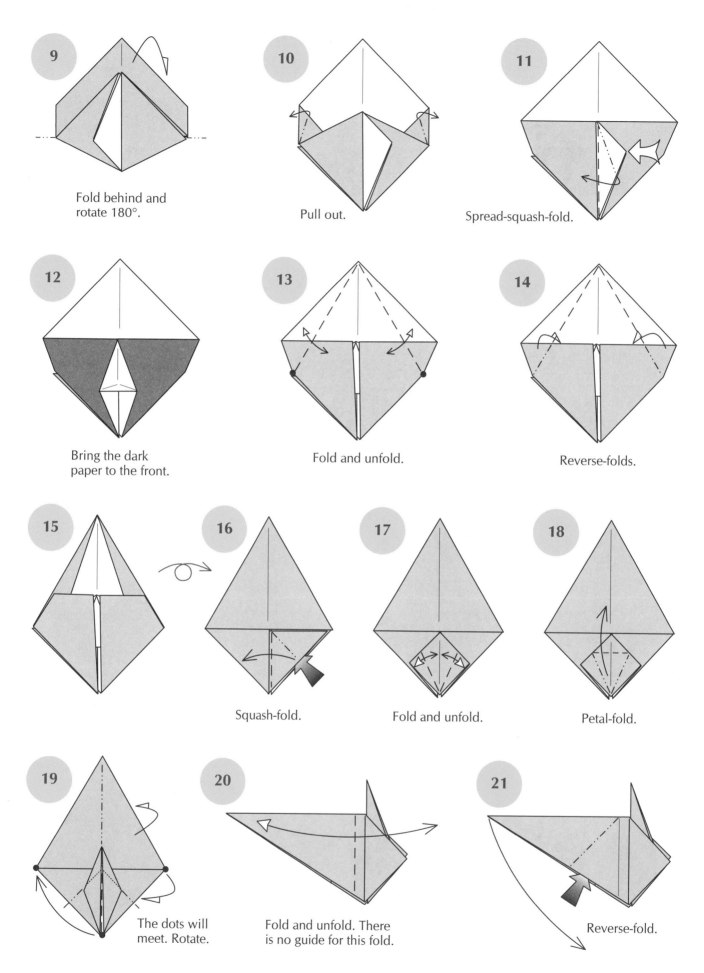

9 Fold behind and rotate 180°.

10 Pull out.

11 Spread-squash-fold.

12 Bring the dark paper to the front.

13 Fold and unfold.

14 Reverse-folds.

15

16 Squash-fold.

17 Fold and unfold.

18 Petal-fold.

19 The dots will meet. Rotate.

20 Fold and unfold. There is no guide for this fold.

21 Reverse-fold.

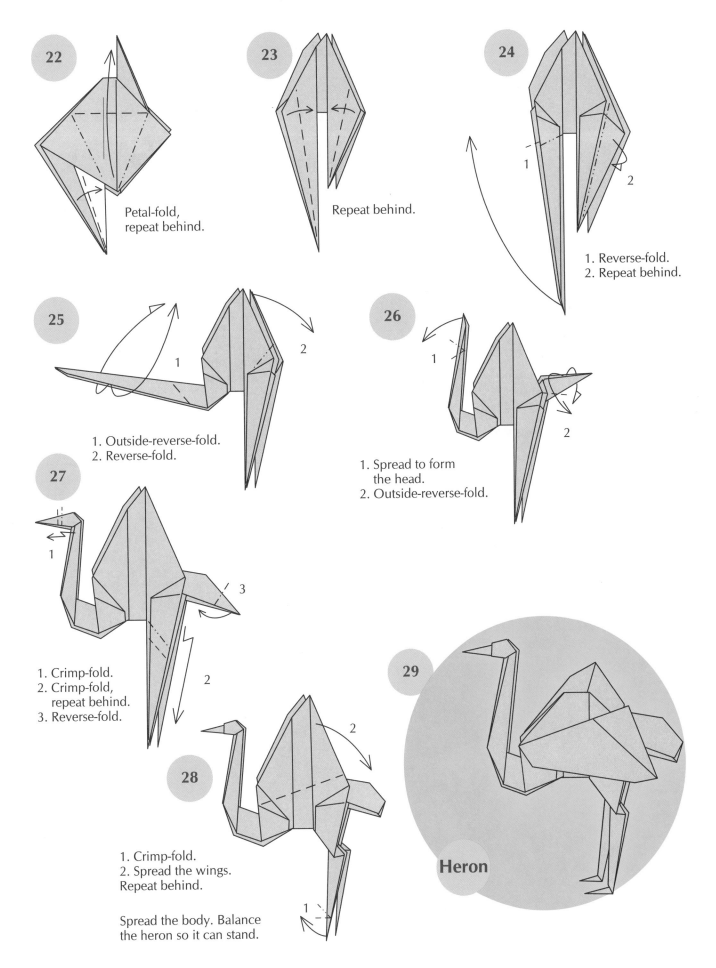

22

Petal-fold,
repeat behind.

23

Repeat behind.

24

1. Reverse-fold.
2. Repeat behind.

25

1. Outside-reverse-fold.
2. Reverse-fold.

26

1. Spread to form
   the head.
2. Outside-reverse-fold.

27

1. Crimp-fold.
2. Crimp-fold,
   repeat behind.
3. Reverse-fold.

28

1. Crimp-fold.
2. Spread the wings.
Repeat behind.

Spread the body. Balance
the heron so it can stand.

29

Heron

Hoopoe

The hoopoe, a relative of the hornbill, lives in the warmer portions of Europe, Asia, and Africa. It is most easily distinguished by a handsome crest of feathers which adorns the top of its head and which it raises and lowers when disturbed. Hoopoes build their nests in trees, wall, and rocks. The female lays 5 to 7 white eggs. While hatching her eggs, the female is fed by the male so she does not have to leave the nest. Hoopoes eat insects, spending much time on the ground searching for them. When frightened, the hoopoe flattens itself to the ground and plays dead.

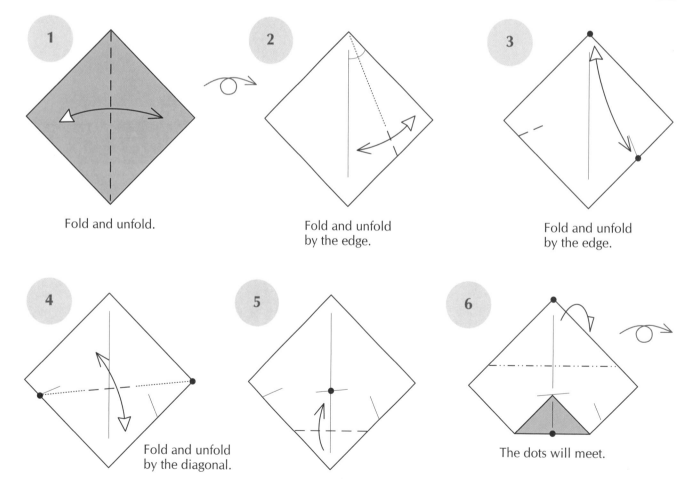

1 Fold and unfold.

2 Fold and unfold by the edge.

3 Fold and unfold by the edge.

4 Fold and unfold by the diagonal.

5

6 The dots will meet.

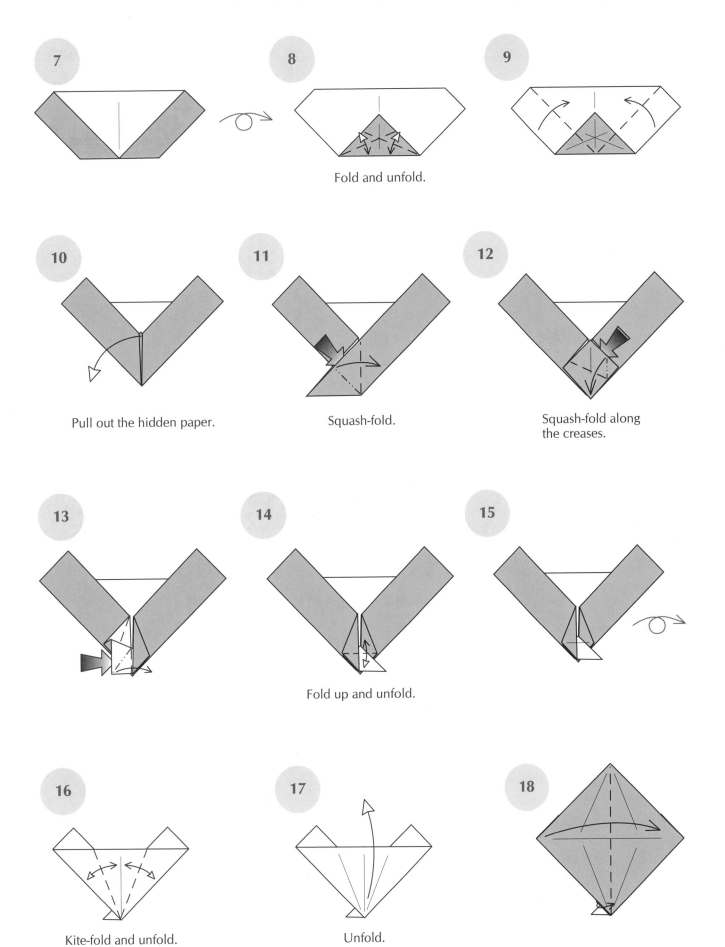

7

8

Fold and unfold.

9

10

Pull out the hidden paper.

11

Squash-fold.

12

Squash-fold along
the creases.

13

14

Fold up and unfold.

15

16

Kite-fold and unfold.

17

Unfold.

18

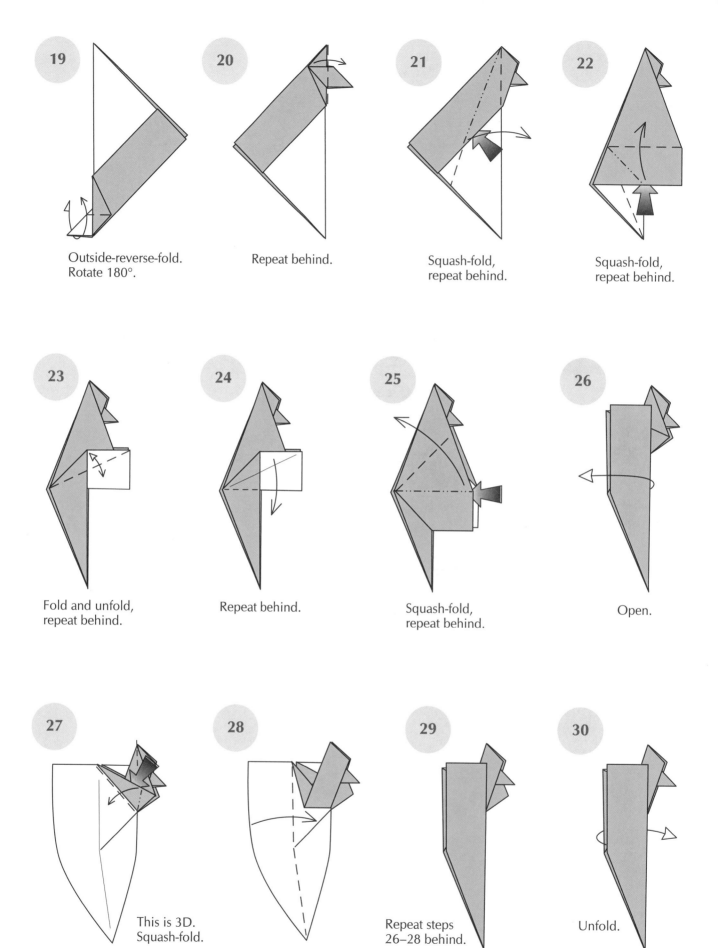

19 Outside-reverse-fold. Rotate 180°.

20 Repeat behind.

21 Squash-fold, repeat behind.

22 Squash-fold, repeat behind.

23 Fold and unfold, repeat behind.

24 Repeat behind.

25 Squash-fold, repeat behind.

26 Open.

27 This is 3D. Squash-fold.

28

29 Repeat steps 26–28 behind.

30 Unfold.

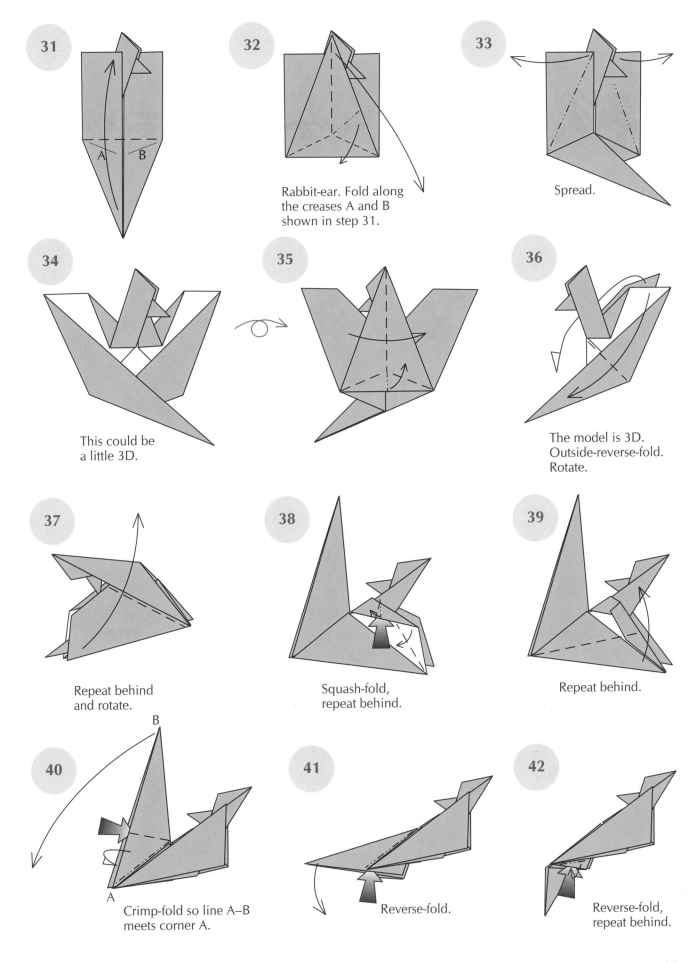

31

32 Rabbit-ear. Fold along the creases A and B shown in step 31.

33 Spread.

34 This could be a little 3D.

35

36 The model is 3D. Outside-reverse-fold. Rotate.

37 Repeat behind and rotate.

38 Squash-fold, repeat behind.

39 Repeat behind.

40 Crimp-fold so line A–B meets corner A.

41 Reverse-fold.

42 Reverse-fold, repeat behind.

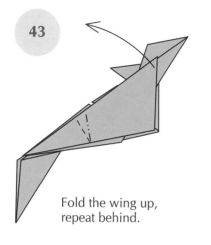

43

Fold the wing up,
repeat behind.

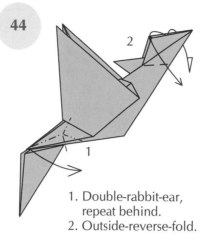

44

1. Double-rabbit-ear,
   repeat behind.
2. Outside-reverse-fold.

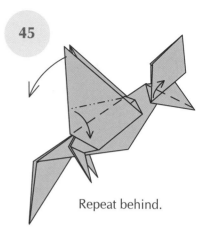

45

Repeat behind.

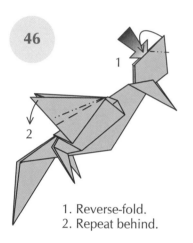

46

1. Reverse-fold.
2. Repeat behind.

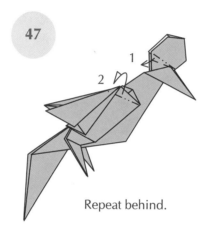

47

Repeat behind.

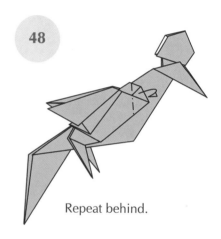

48

Repeat behind.

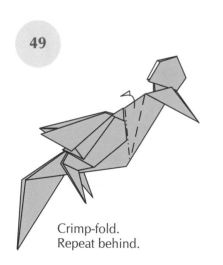

49

Crimp-fold.
Repeat behind.

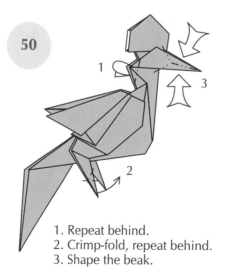

50

1. Repeat behind.
2. Crimp-fold, repeat behind.
3. Shape the beak.

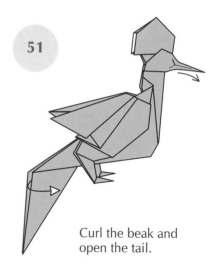

51

Curl the beak and
open the tail.

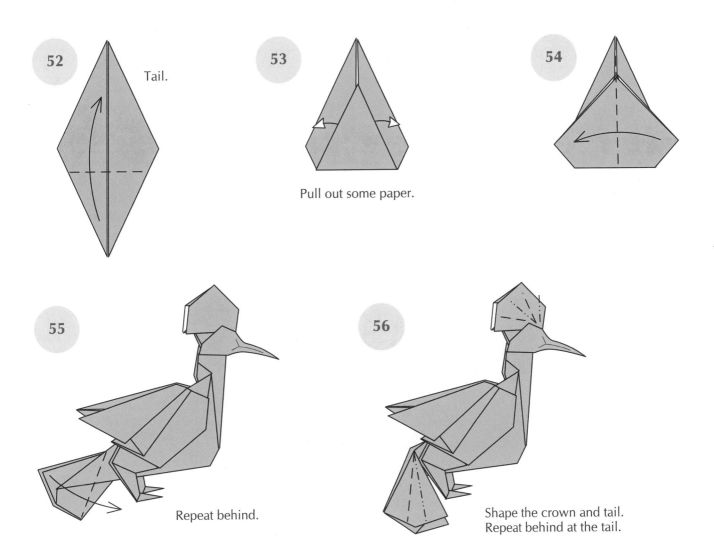

52 Tail.

53 Pull out some paper.

54

55 Repeat behind.

56 Shape the crown and tail. Repeat behind at the tail.

57

Hoopoe

Hummingbird

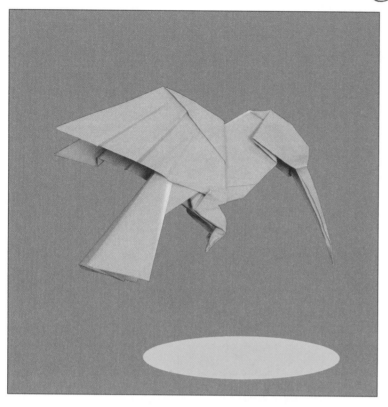

Hummingbirds are amongst the smallest birds in the world, measuring from only three to five inches and are named after the sound their wings make when moving at very high speeds. Hummingbirds are found in the Americas from Alaska all the way to Argentina.

Begin with step 29 of the Anhinga (page 15).

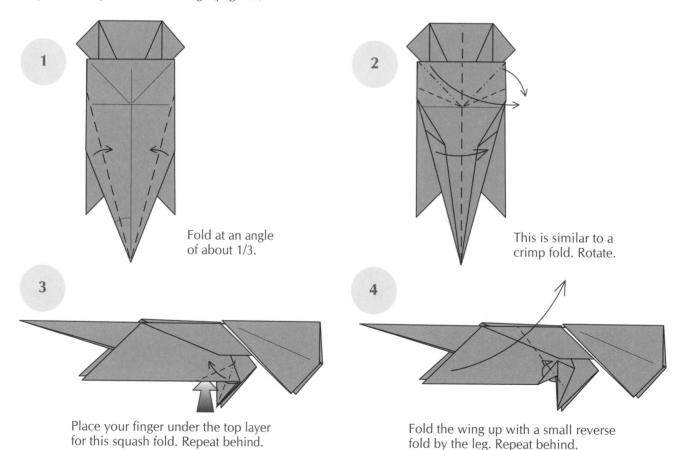

1 Fold at an angle of about 1/3.

2 This is similar to a crimp fold. Rotate.

3 Place your finger under the top layer for this squash fold. Repeat behind.

4 Fold the wing up with a small reverse fold by the leg. Repeat behind.

5

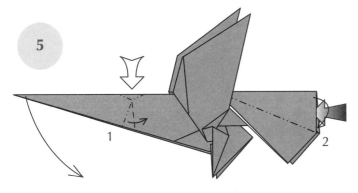

1. This is similar to a crimp fold.
2. Reverse-fold.

6

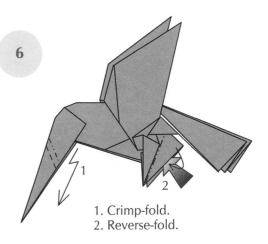

1. Crimp-fold.
2. Reverse-fold.

7

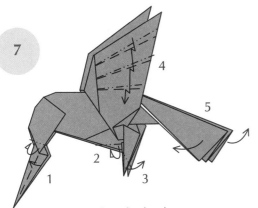

1. Thin the beak.
2. Fold inside.
3. Reverse-fold.
4. Pleat the wings.
5. Spread the tail.
Repeat behind.

8

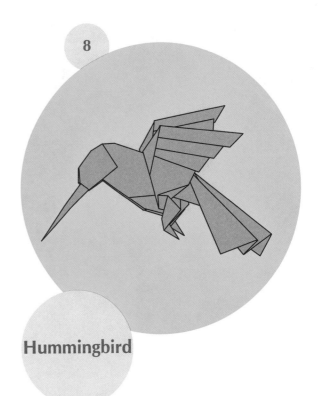

Hummingbird

Ibis

Ibises are long-legged birds that spend much of their time around marshes and swamps. With their long curved bills, they can catch frogs, snakes, insects, and other small animals. Though usually quiet birds, they can make harsh croaking sounds if provoked. These social birds nest and fly in groups. The ibis was considered to be sacred to the ancient Egyptians.

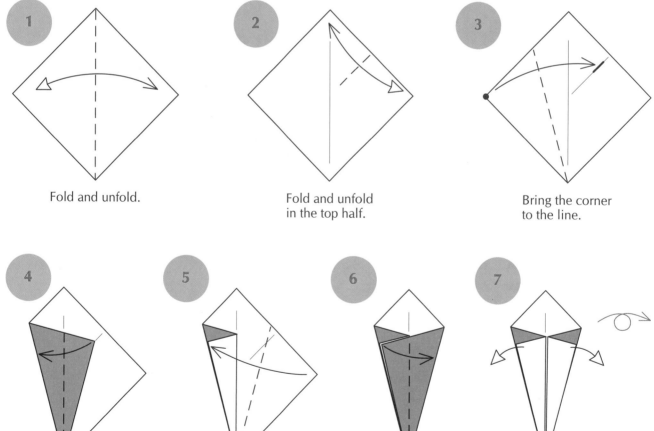

1 Fold and unfold.

2 Fold and unfold in the top half.

3 Bring the corner to the line.

4

5

6

7 Unfold.

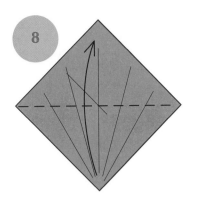

8

9

Only crease a
little on the left.

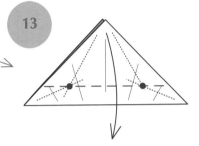

10

Unfold.

11

Fold and unfold.

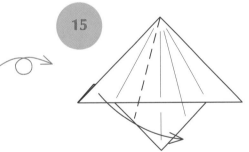

12

Note the dots.

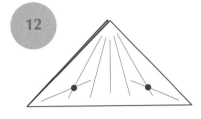

13

Fold down by the
intersections of the
hidden layer.

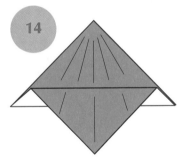

14

15

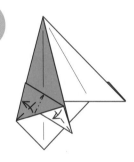

16

Squash-fold.

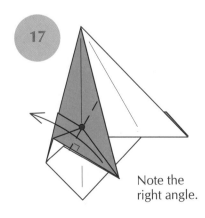

17

Note the
right angle.

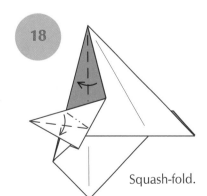

18

Squash-fold.

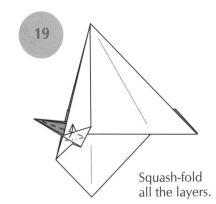

19

Squash-fold
all the layers.

Ibis 71

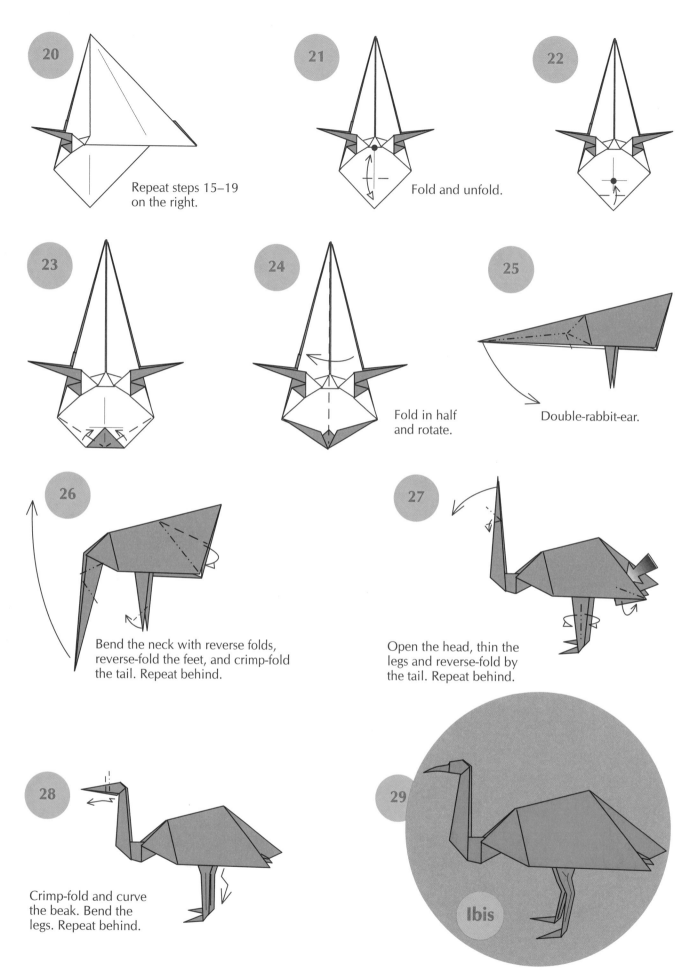

20 Repeat steps 15–19 on the right.

21 Fold and unfold.

22

23

24 Fold in half and rotate.

25 Double-rabbit-ear.

26 Bend the neck with reverse folds, reverse-fold the feet, and crimp-fold the tail. Repeat behind.

27 Open the head, thin the legs and reverse-fold by the tail. Repeat behind.

28 Crimp-fold and curve the beak. Bend the legs. Repeat behind.

29 Ibis

Sacred Ibis

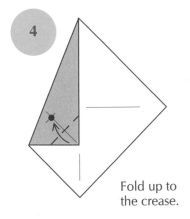

The sacred ibis is naturally found in sub-Saharan Africa, Iraq, and Egypt although it has been introduced to France, Italy, Spain, Taiwan, and the United States. A full grown Sacred Ibis is about 27 inches long. The ancient Egyptians worshiped the sacred ibis in the form of the god Thoth.

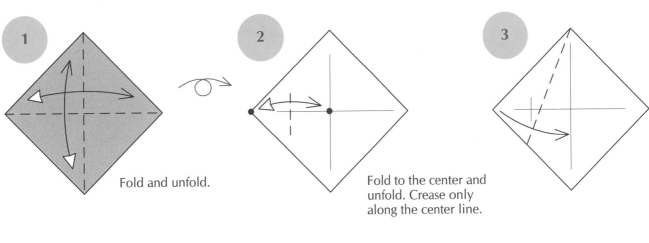

1 Fold and unfold.

2 Fold to the center and unfold. Crease only along the center line.

3

4 Fold up to the crease.

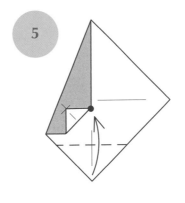

5

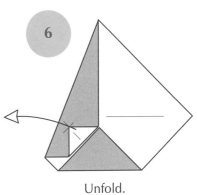

6 Unfold.

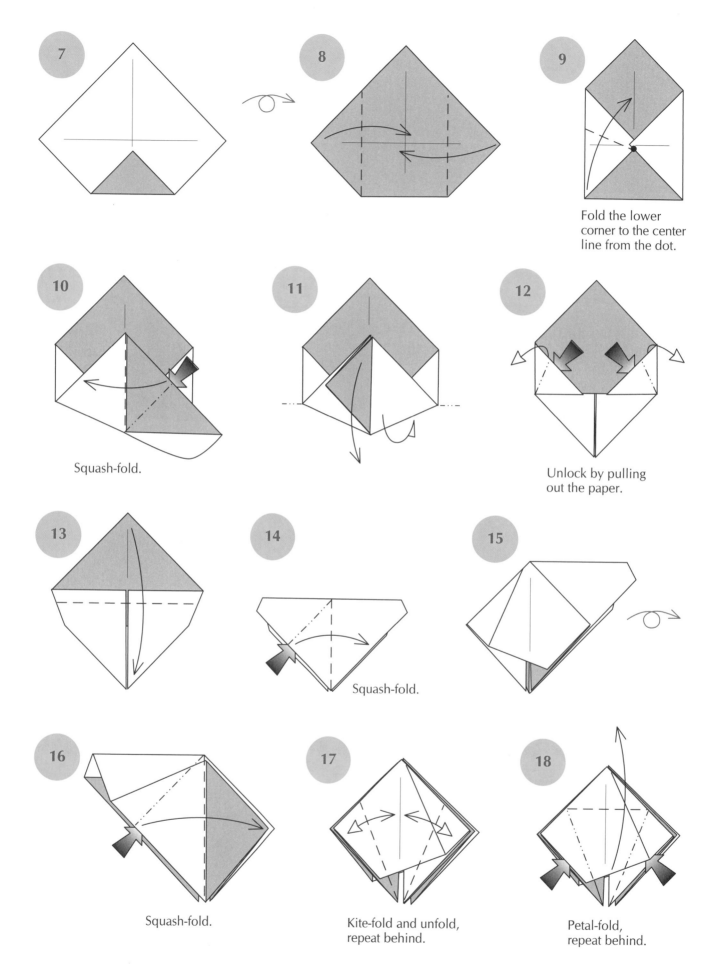

9 Fold the lower corner to the center line from the dot.

10 Squash-fold.

12 Unlock by pulling out the paper.

14 Squash-fold.

16 Squash-fold.

17 Kite-fold and unfold, repeat behind.

18 Petal-fold, repeat behind.

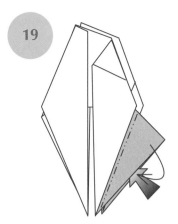

19

Reverse-fold.

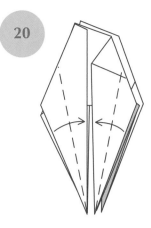

20

Repeat behind.

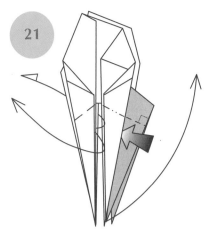

21

Outside-reverse-fold the neck to reverse colors. Reverse-fold the legs at a right angle.

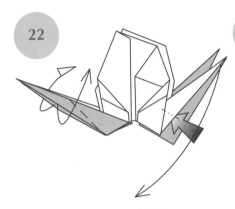

22

Outside-reverse-fold the neck. Reverse-fold the legs.

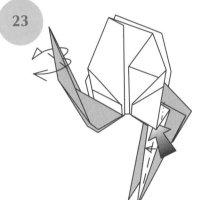

23

Outside-reverse-fold the head. Thin the white layer of the leg, repeat behind.

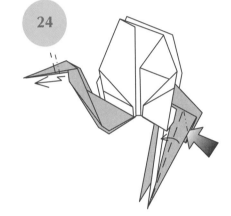

24

Crimp-fold to form the beak. Squash-fold to thin the leg, repeat behind.

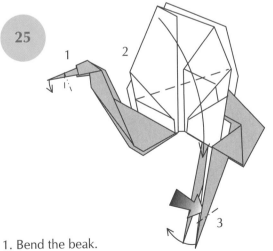

25

1. Bend the beak.
2. Fold the wings down.
3. Reverse-fold the feet and adjust them so the ibis can stand.

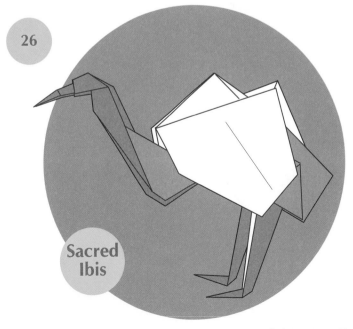

26

Sacred Ibis

Ostrich

The ostrich is a large flightless bird that is indigenous to Africa. It has long legs and a long neck and is able to run at speeds up to 43 mph. Male Ostriches can weigh up to 300 pounds and stand over 9 feet tall. Their diet consists mainly of seeds, grass, fruit, and occasionally insects such as locusts.

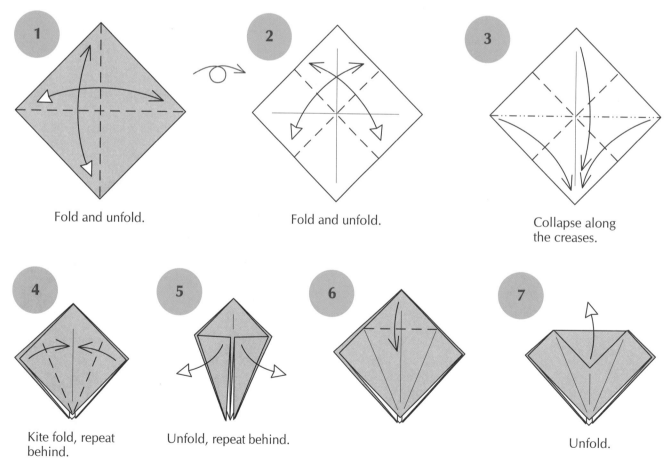

1 Fold and unfold.

2 Fold and unfold.

3 Collapse along the creases.

4 Kite fold, repeat behind.

5 Unfold, repeat behind.

6

7 Unfold.

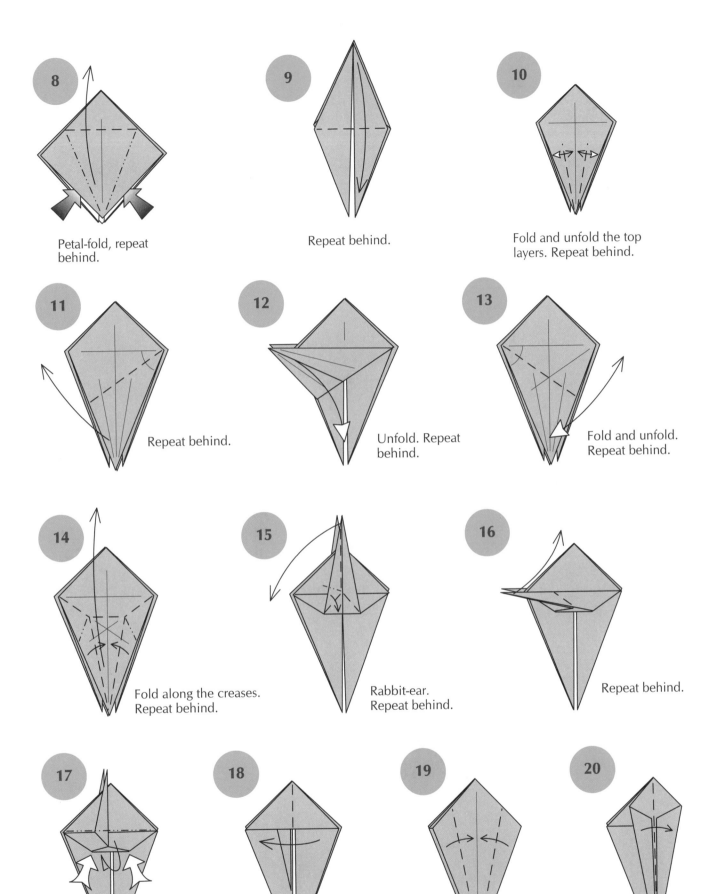

8 Petal-fold, repeat behind.

9 Repeat behind.

10 Fold and unfold the top layers. Repeat behind.

11 Repeat behind.

12 Unfold. Repeat behind.

13 Fold and unfold. Repeat behind.

14 Fold along the creases. Repeat behind.

15 Rabbit-ear. Repeat behind.

16 Repeat behind.

17 Spread the paper to sink. Repeat behind.

18

19

20

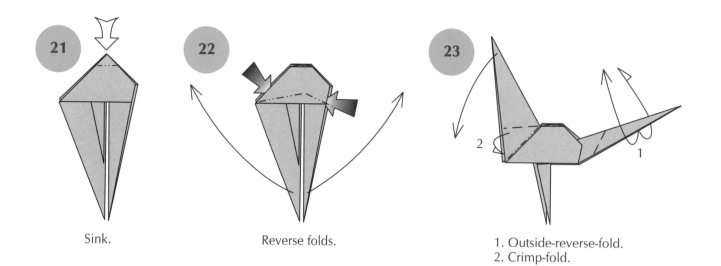

21

Sink.

22

Reverse folds.

23

1. Outside-reverse-fold.
2. Crimp-fold.

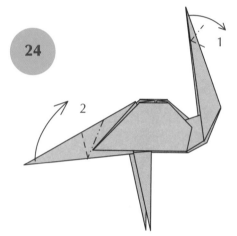

24

1. Spread to form the head.
2. Crimp-fold.

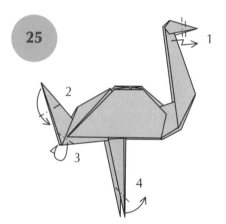

25

1. Crimp-fold.
2. Reverse-fold.
3. Repeat behind.
4. Reverse-fold, repeat behind.

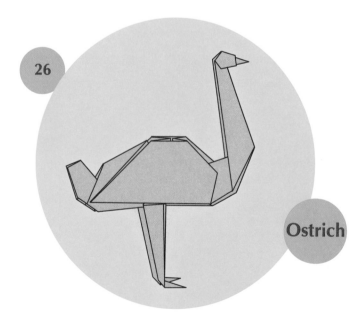

26

Ostrich

Owl

Owls represent wisdom in mythology and popular culture. There are about 205 species of owls ranging in size from 5 to 33 inches. Owls have large eyes facing the front which gives them depth perception. Although owls have very good vision, their large eyes are fixed in their sockets, so they have to turn their entire head to change views. They can rotate their heads and necks by as much as 270 degrees. Their night vision is especially good. The owl has a short, pointed beak and sharp, curved claws.

1 Fold and unfold.

2 Kite-fold.

3

4 Fold and unfold the top layer.

5 Rabbit-ear.

6 Squash-fold.

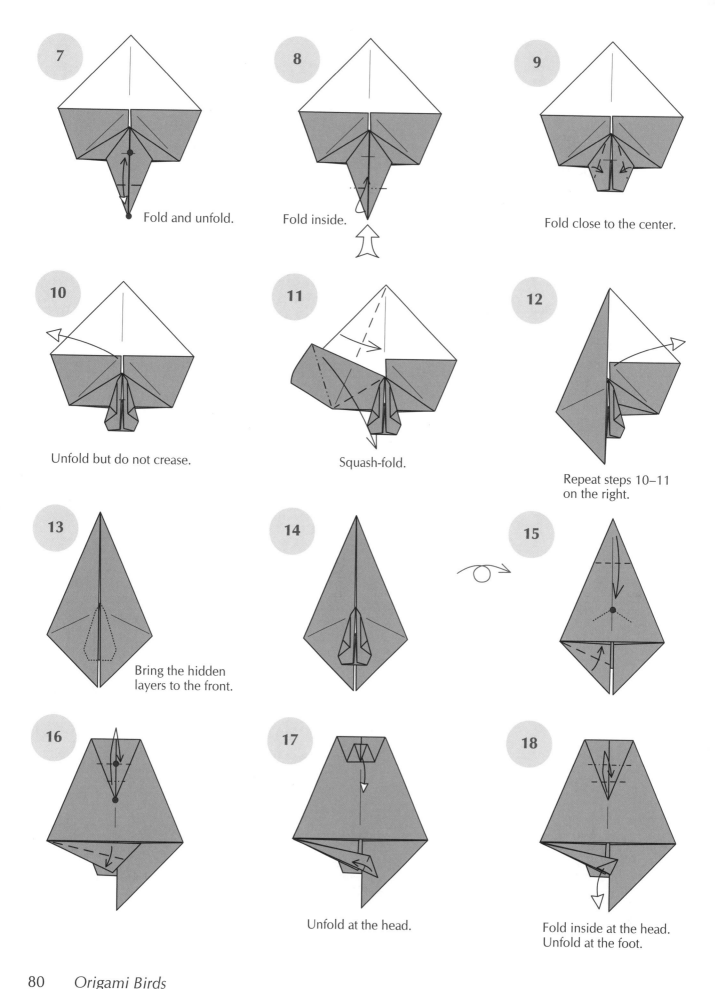

7 Fold and unfold.

8 Fold inside.

9 Fold close to the center.

10 Unfold but do not crease.

11 Squash-fold.

12 Repeat steps 10–11 on the right.

13 Bring the hidden layers to the front.

14

15

16

17 Unfold at the head.

18 Fold inside at the head. Unfold at the foot.

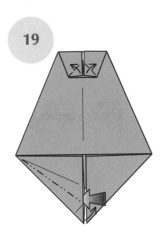

19

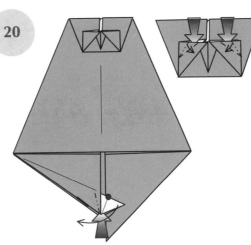

20

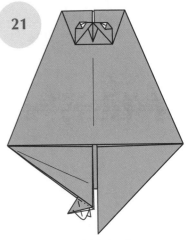

21

Reverse-fold at the bottom.

Squash-fold the eyes. Reverse-fold at the bottom so the dot meets the line.

Crimp-fold the foot.

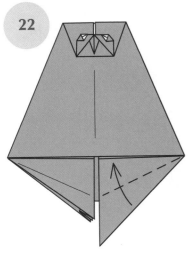

22

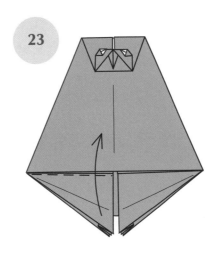

23

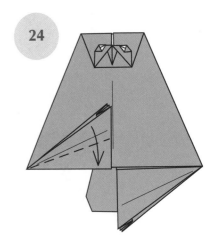

24

Repeat steps 15–21 on the right at the bottom.

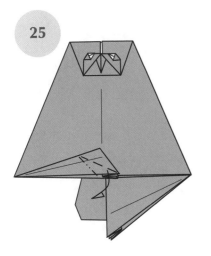

25

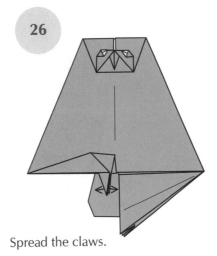

26

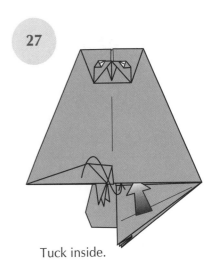

27

Spread the claws.

Tuck inside.

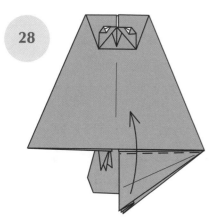

28

Repeat steps 23–27
on the right.

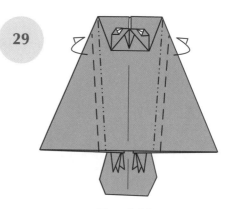

29

Pleat folds.

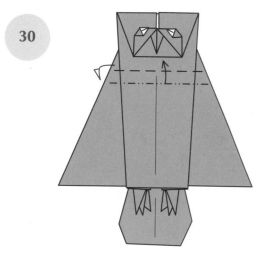

30

Pleat-fold.

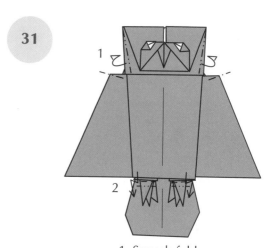

31

1. Squash folds.
2. Pleat folds.

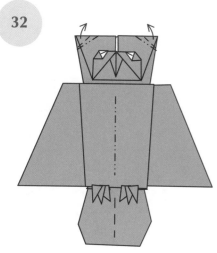

32

Shape the ears, body, and tail.

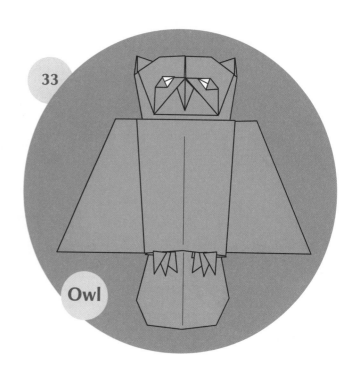

33

Owl

Parrot

The term "parrot" is a general one that applies to about 300 different species. Parrots are for the most part mild mannered; however some species have been known to attack sheep and damage crops. In general, these elegant creatures live in warm, tropical climates and feed on fruits and seeds, among other treats.

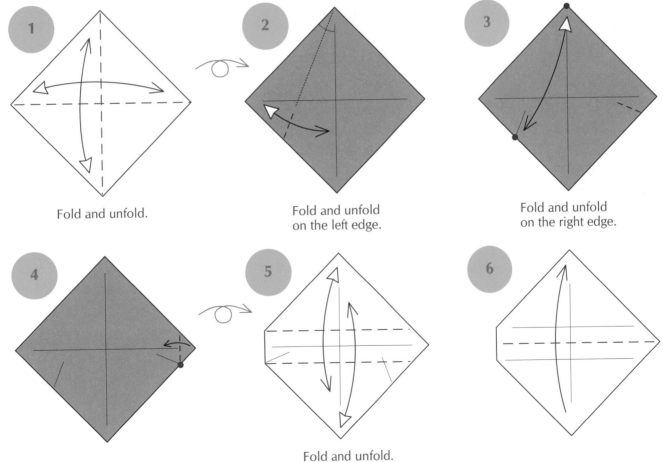

1 Fold and unfold.

2 Fold and unfold on the left edge.

3 Fold and unfold on the right edge.

4

5 Fold and unfold.

6

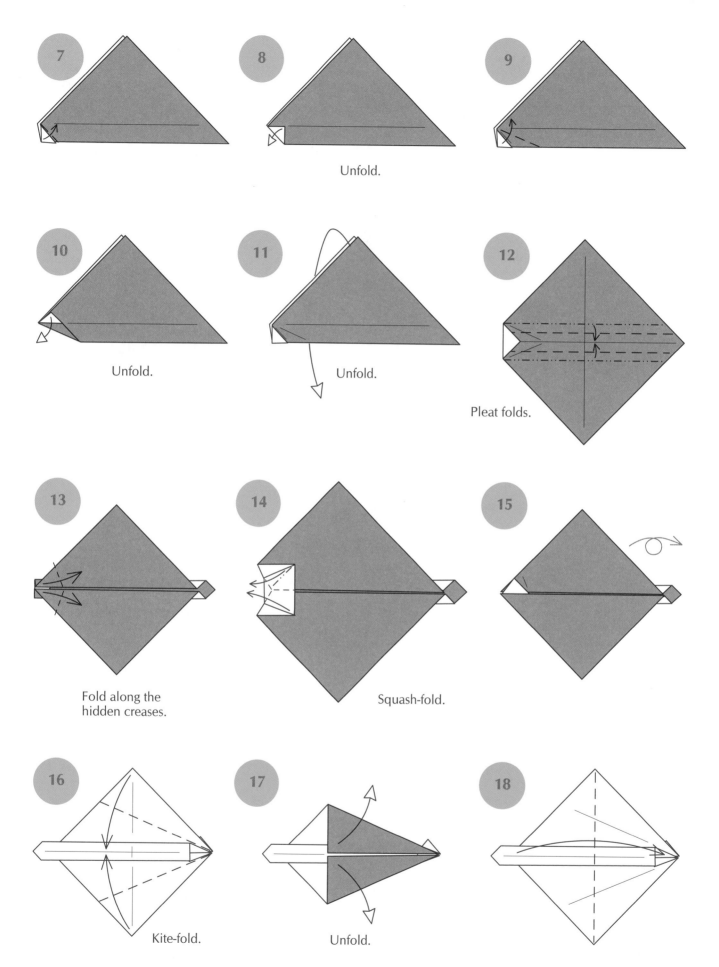

7

8

Unfold.

9

10

Unfold.

11

Unfold.

12

Pleat folds.

13

Fold along the
hidden creases.

14

Squash-fold.

15

16

Kite-fold.

17

Unfold.

18

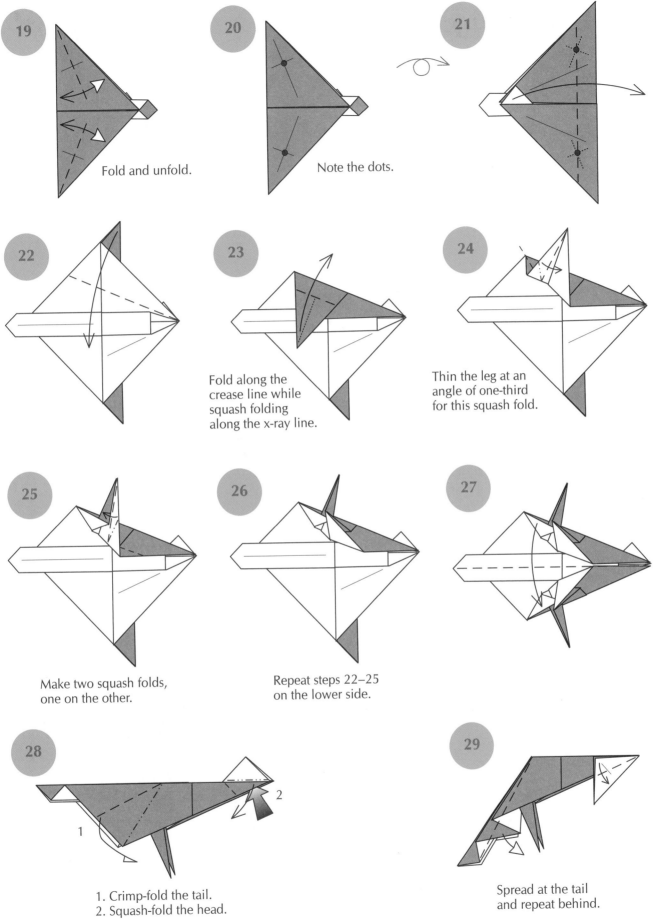

19 Fold and unfold.

20 Note the dots.

21

22

23 Fold along the crease line while squash folding along the x-ray line.

24 Thin the leg at an angle of one-third for this squash fold.

25 Make two squash folds, one on the other.

26 Repeat steps 22–25 on the lower side.

27

28
1. Crimp-fold the tail.
2. Squash-fold the head.

29 Spread at the tail and repeat behind.

Parrot 85

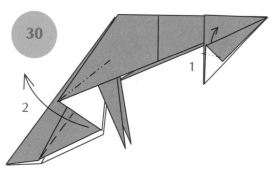

30

1. Reverse-fold the beak.
2. Reverse-fold the tail, repeat behind.

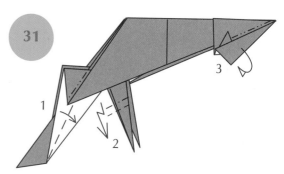

31

1. Reverse-fold the tail.
2. Crimp-fold the legs.
3. Tuck inside at the head. Repeat behind.

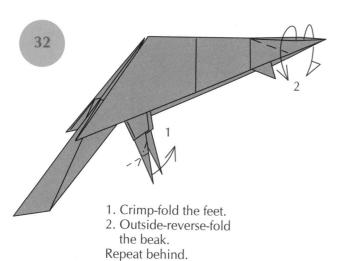

32

1. Crimp-fold the feet.
2. Outside-reverse-fold the beak. Repeat behind.

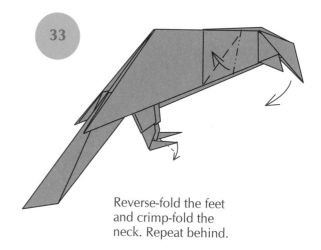

33

Reverse-fold the feet and crimp-fold the neck. Repeat behind.

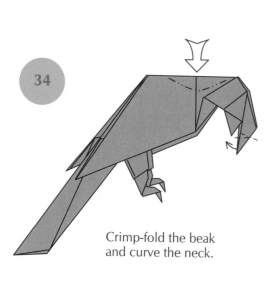

34

Crimp-fold the beak and curve the neck.

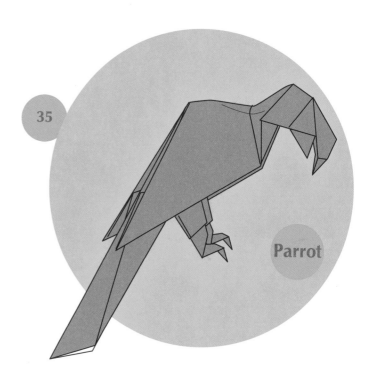

35

Parrot

Peacock

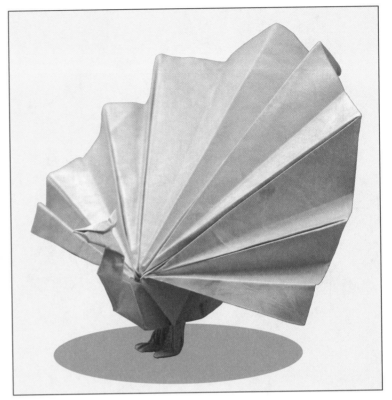

The peacock, which is the male peafowl, has distinctive plumage and an elegant head crest. In full plumage it is about seven feet tall. The plumes, which are long feathers, are not the tail. It lives by river banks, forest clearings, or other places with scattered trees. It flies quite well and travels in small flocks. The peacock feeds on seeds and grasses.

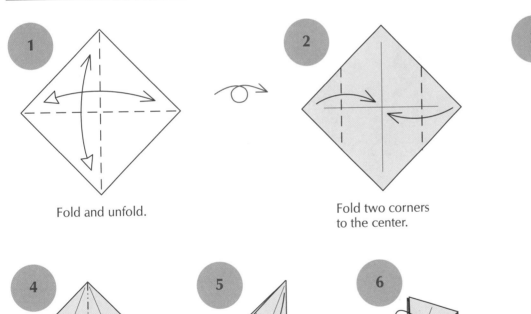

1
Fold and unfold.

2
Fold two corners to the center.

3
Fold and unfold.

4

5

6

7
Squash-fold and rotate.

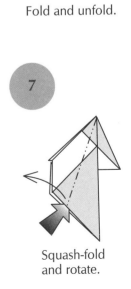

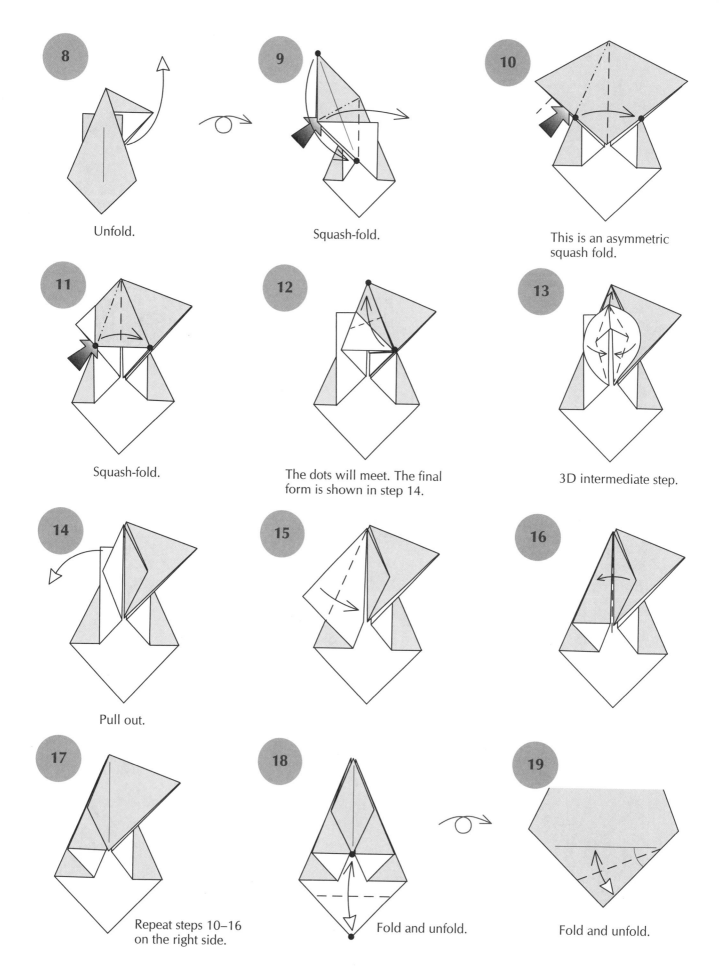

8 Unfold.

9 Squash-fold.

10 This is an asymmetric squash fold.

11 Squash-fold.

12 The dots will meet. The final form is shown in step 14.

13 3D intermediate step.

14 Pull out.

15

16

17 Repeat steps 10–16 on the right side.

18 Fold and unfold.

19 Fold and unfold.

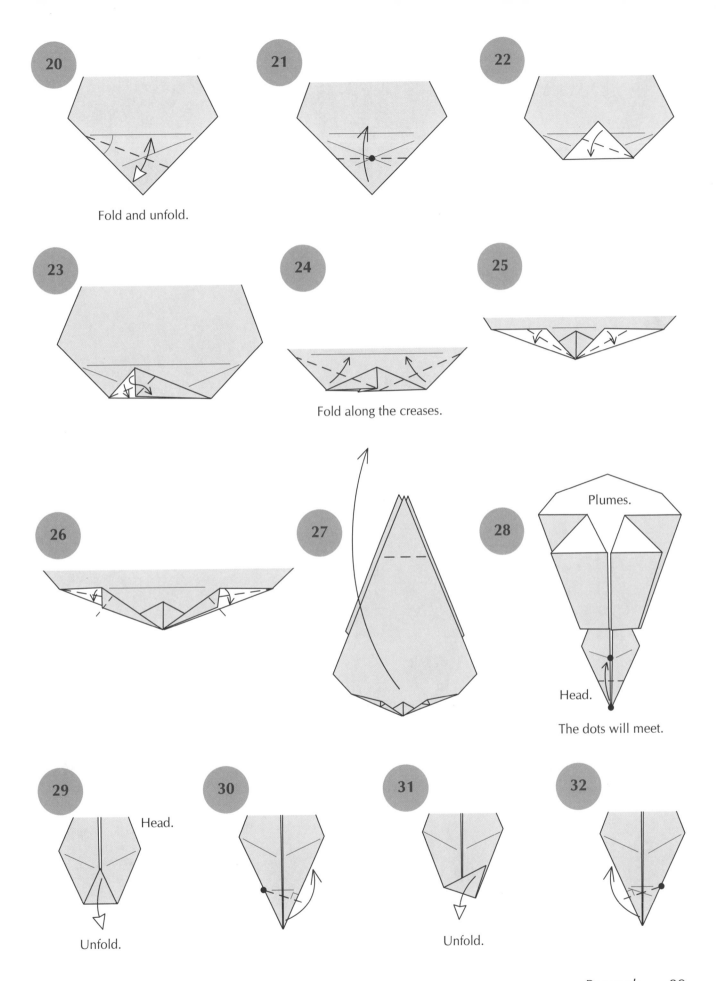

20
Fold and unfold.

21

22

23

24
Fold along the creases.

25

26

27

28
Plumes.

Head.

The dots will meet.

29
Head.

Unfold.

30

31
Unfold.

32

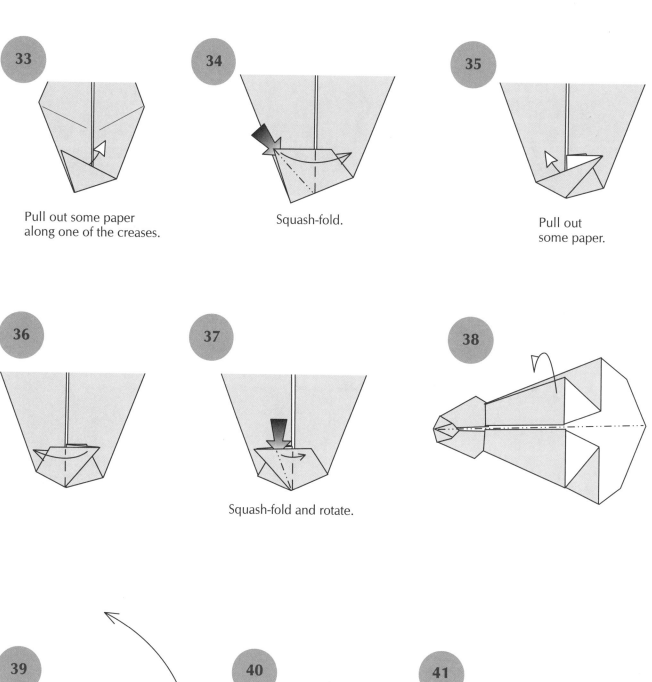

33 Pull out some paper along one of the creases.

34 Squash-fold.

35 Pull out some paper.

36

37 Squash-fold and rotate.

38

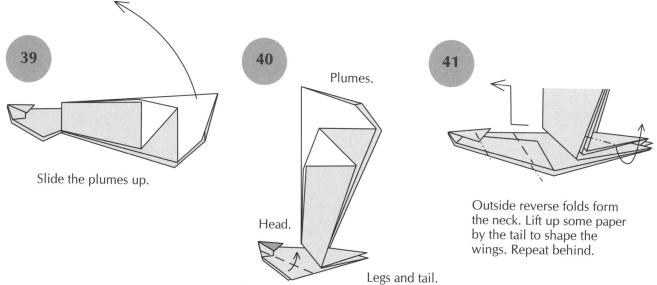

39 Slide the plumes up.

40 Plumes.

Head.

Legs and tail.

Fold up so that it is under the darker paper. Repeat behind.

41 Outside reverse folds form the neck. Lift up some paper by the tail to shape the wings. Repeat behind.

42

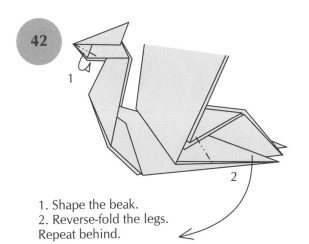

1. Shape the beak.
2. Reverse-fold the legs.
Repeat behind.

43

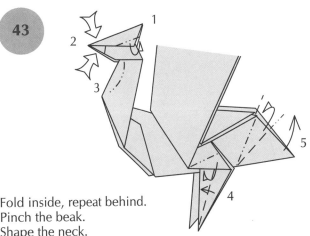

1. Fold inside, repeat behind.
2. Pinch the beak.
3. Shape the neck.
4. Thin the leg, repeat on the other side, and repeat on the other leg.
5. This is similar to a crimp fold, it forms the tail and wings.

44

Leg.

Crimp-fold the leg.
Repeat behind.

45

Plumes.

Repeat behind.

46

Repeat behind.

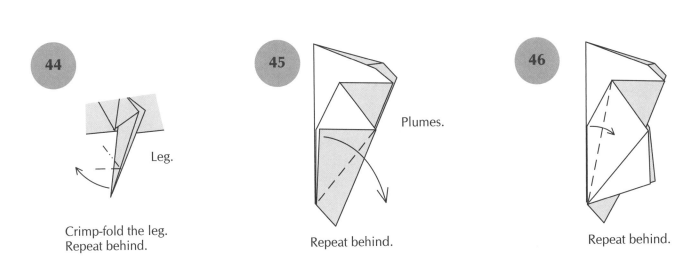

47

Repeat behind.

48

Repeat behind.

49

Sink. Repeat behind.

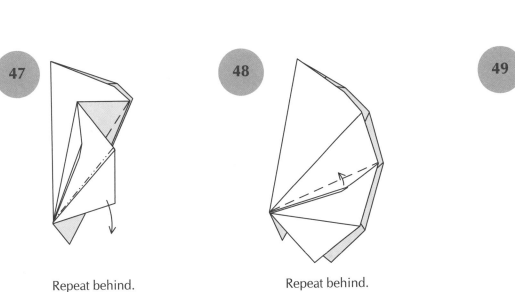
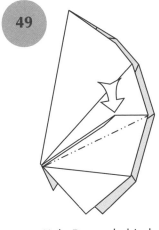

50 Crimp-fold.

51 Repeat behind.

52 Repeat behind.

53 Repeat behind.

54 Unfold, repeat behind.

55 Spread the plumes.

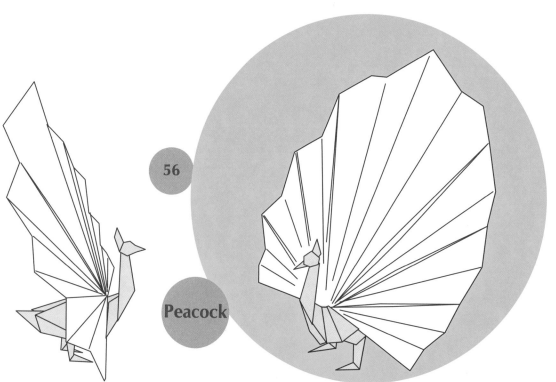

56

Peacock

Pelican

The pelican is a large water bird characterized by a large beak with an elastic pouch that is used to catch fish, its main food source. The beak can hold two to three gallons of water. Pelicans weigh about thirty pounds and can have wingspans of up to ten feet, allowing them to reach heights of about 10,000 feet.

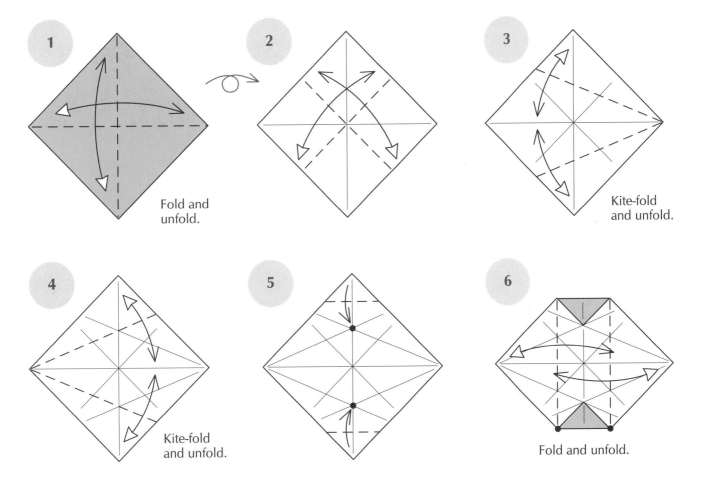

1. Fold and unfold.

2.

3. Kite-fold and unfold.

4. Kite-fold and unfold.

5.

6. Fold and unfold.

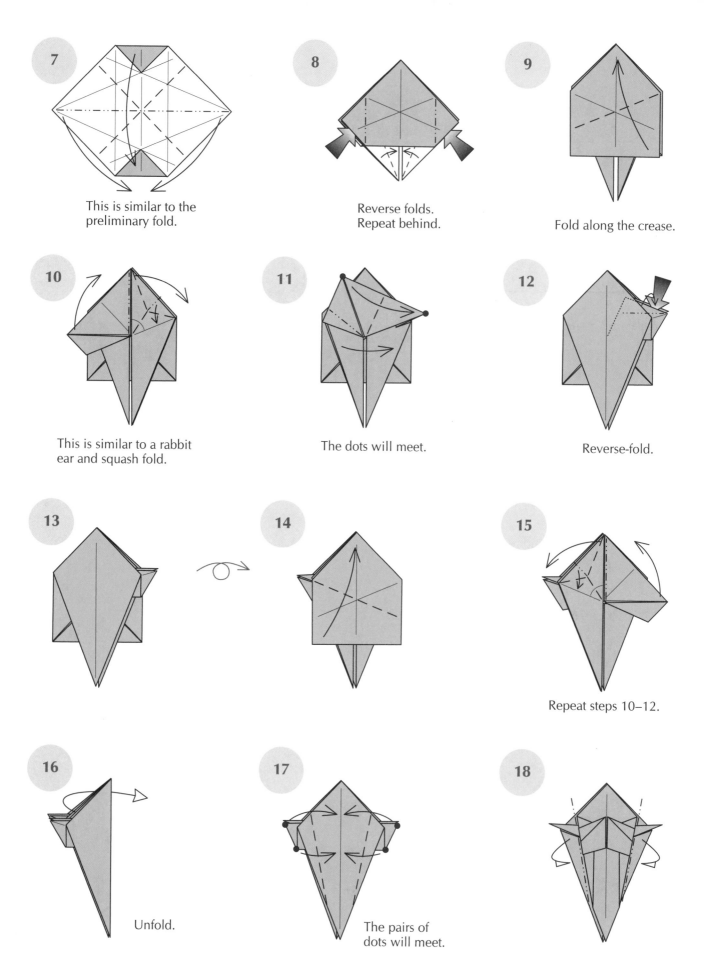

7 This is similar to the preliminary fold.

8 Reverse folds. Repeat behind.

9 Fold along the crease.

10 This is similar to a rabbit ear and squash fold.

11 The dots will meet.

12 Reverse-fold.

13

14

15 Repeat steps 10–12.

16 Unfold.

17 The pairs of dots will meet.

18

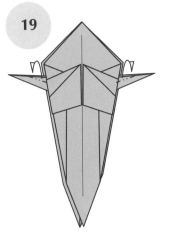

19

Fold inside and
repeat behind.

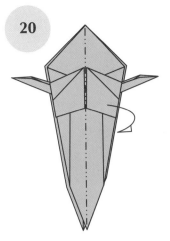

20

Fold in half and rotate.

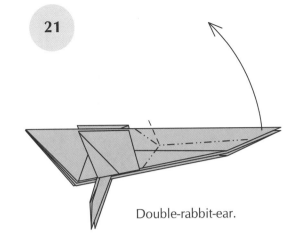

21

Double-rabbit-ear.

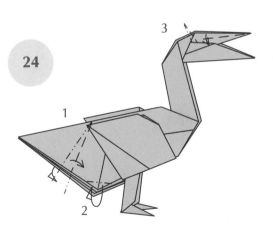

22

1. Reverse-fold, repeat behind.
2. Reverse-fold.

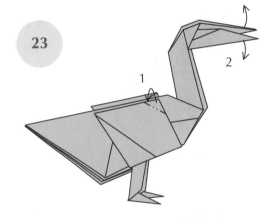

23

1. Reverse-fold, repeat behind.
2. Spread.

24

1. Crimp-fold.
2. Fold the layers inside. Repeat behind.
3. Shape the beak and eye. Repeat beind.

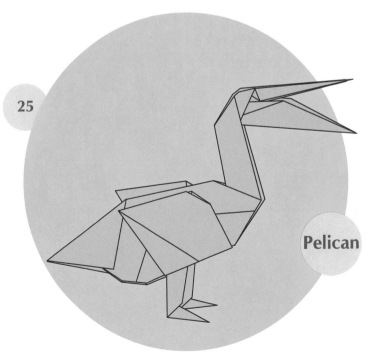

25

Pelican

Penguin

The penguin is an aquatic, flightless bird that lives in Antarctica. Well-adapted to the water, on land, it can run, hop, or slide on its belly. The adult is from one to four feet tall and weighs from 4 to 90 pounds. Penguins feed on fish, squid and other sea-creatures.

1

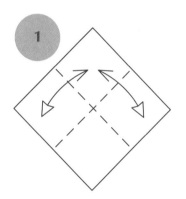

Fold and unfold.

2

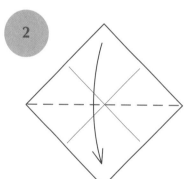

3

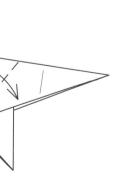

Reverse-fold.

4

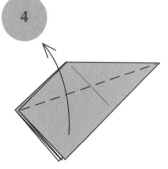

Repeat behind.

5

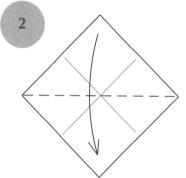

Repeat behind.

6

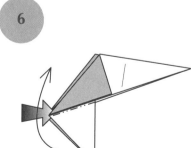

Reverse-fold and rotate.

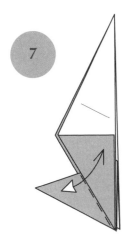

7

Fold and unfold.

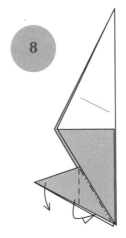

8

Crimp-fold.

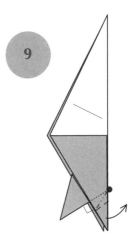

9

Note the right angle.
Crimp-fold and
repeat behind.

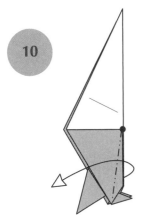

10

Unlock and pull out the top
layer. If it does not meet at
the dot, then adjust the crimp
fold in step 9. Repeat behind.

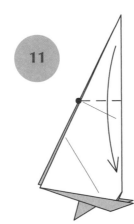

11

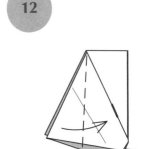

12

Fold close to
the bold edge.
Repeat behind.

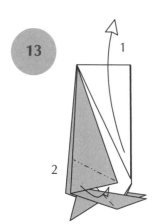

13

1. Unfold.
2. Reverse-fold,
   repeat behind.
Rotate.

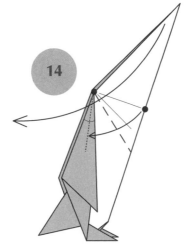

14

Bring the dot on the right to the
center line of the wing. (There
is no crease at the x-ray line.)

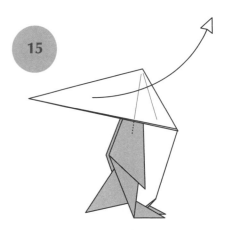

15

Unfold.

16

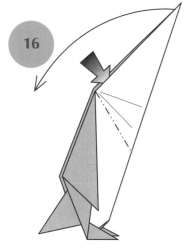

Reverse-fold.

17

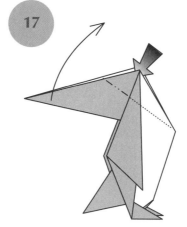

Extra line.

One side has an extra line, it does
not matter which side. Reverse-fold.

18

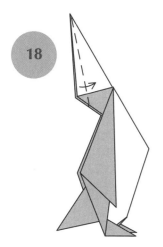

Fold along the hidden
edge. Repeat behind.

19

Outside-reverse-fold.

20

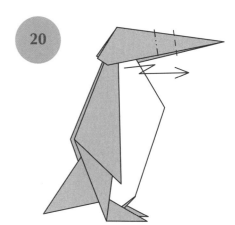

Reverse folds.

21

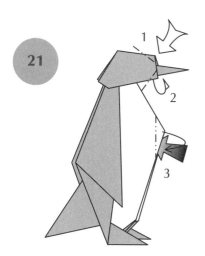

1. Reverse-fold.
2. Mountain-fold, repeat behind.
3. Reverse-fold.

22

Penguin

Baby Penguin

Penguins may come in many species, but they all have their own baby penguins. The parents take turns keeping their egg warm and safe from such predators as gulls who consider penguin eggs a delicacy, and it can take nearly two months for the egg to hatch. The baby penguins tend to have drab fluffy coats in contrast to the well-known solid black and white coats of their parents.

1

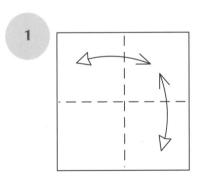

Fold and unfold.

2

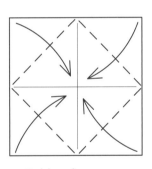

Fold to the center.

3

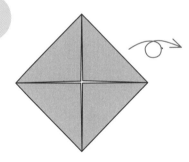

4

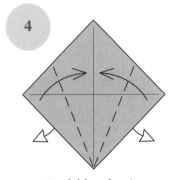

Kite-fold and swing out from behind.

5

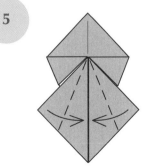

Kite-fold.

6

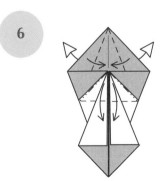

Make squash folds and swing out from behind.

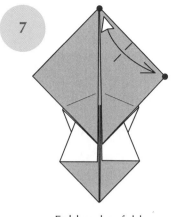

7 Fold and unfold.

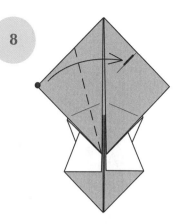

8 Fold the top layer. Bring the dot the to crease.

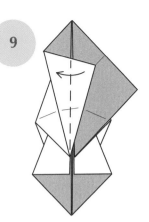

9

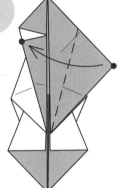

10

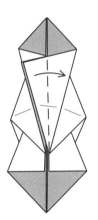

11

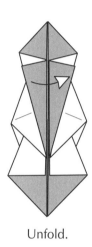

12 Unfold.

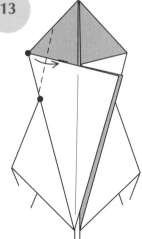

13 The top part is shown. Fold close to the lower dot.

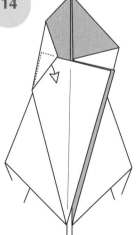

14 Pull out.

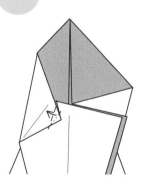

15 Squash-fold the eye.

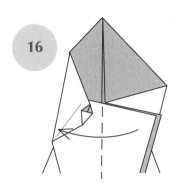

16

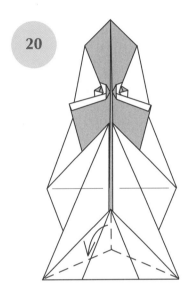

17

Squash-fold so the eye is surrounded by white paper.

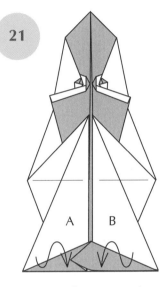

18

Repeat steps 12–17 on the right.

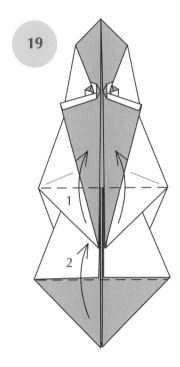

19

1

2

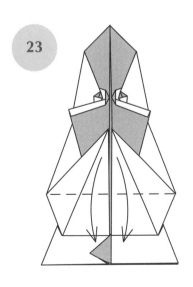

20

Rabbit-ear but do not flatten.

21

A   B

Bring layers A and B to the front.

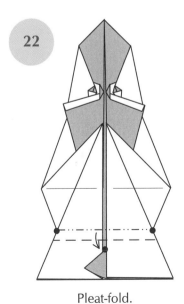

22

Pleat-fold.

23

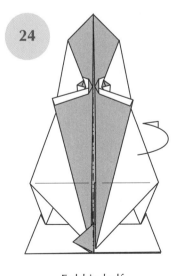

24

Fold in half.

25

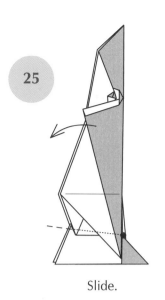

Slide.

26

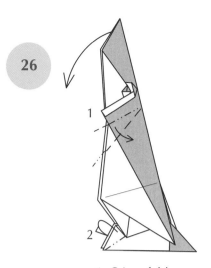

1. Crimp-fold.
2. Repeat behind.

27

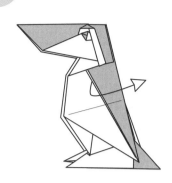

Pull out and repeat behind.

28

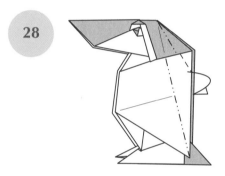

Fold directly behind.
Repeat behind.

29

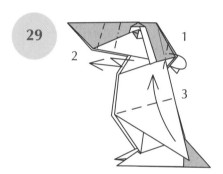

1. Repeat behind.
2. Crimp-fold.
3. Repeat behind.

30

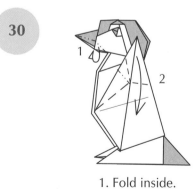

1. Fold inside.
2. Rabbit-ear.
Repeat behind.

31

Baby Penguin

Pigeon

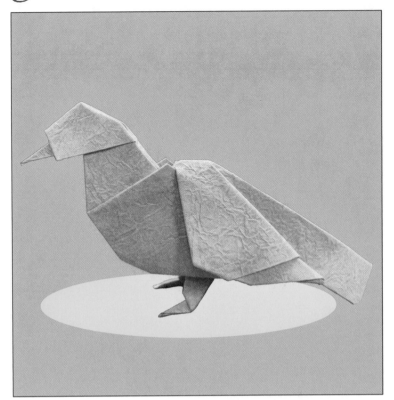

Pigeons are part of the bird family *Columbidae*. A bird in this family will usually have a stout body with a small neck and a small beak. Pigeons dwell in every area of the world except Antarctica, the Arctic, and parts of the Sahara Desert. The bird that people commonly refer to as a pigeon, is the Feral Rock Pigeon. Most people think of doves as certain type of bird, but they are actually just pigeons; the words "pigeon" and "dove" can be used interchangeably. A pigeon's diet mostly consist of seeds and fruits. They usually make their nests in trees.

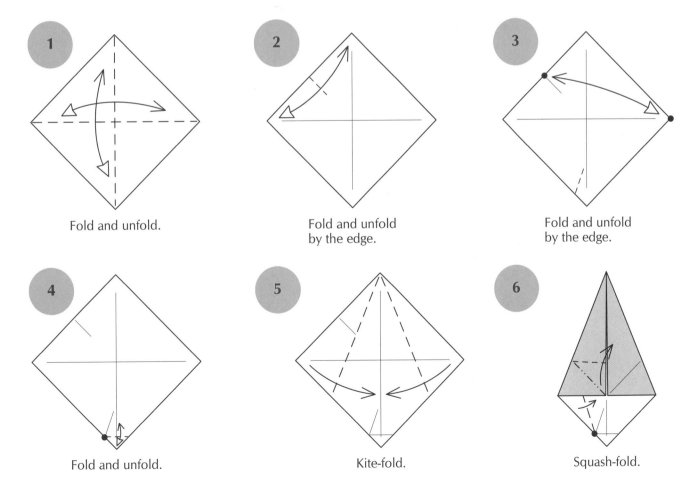

1 Fold and unfold.

2 Fold and unfold by the edge.

3 Fold and unfold by the edge.

4 Fold and unfold.

5 Kite-fold.

6 Squash-fold.

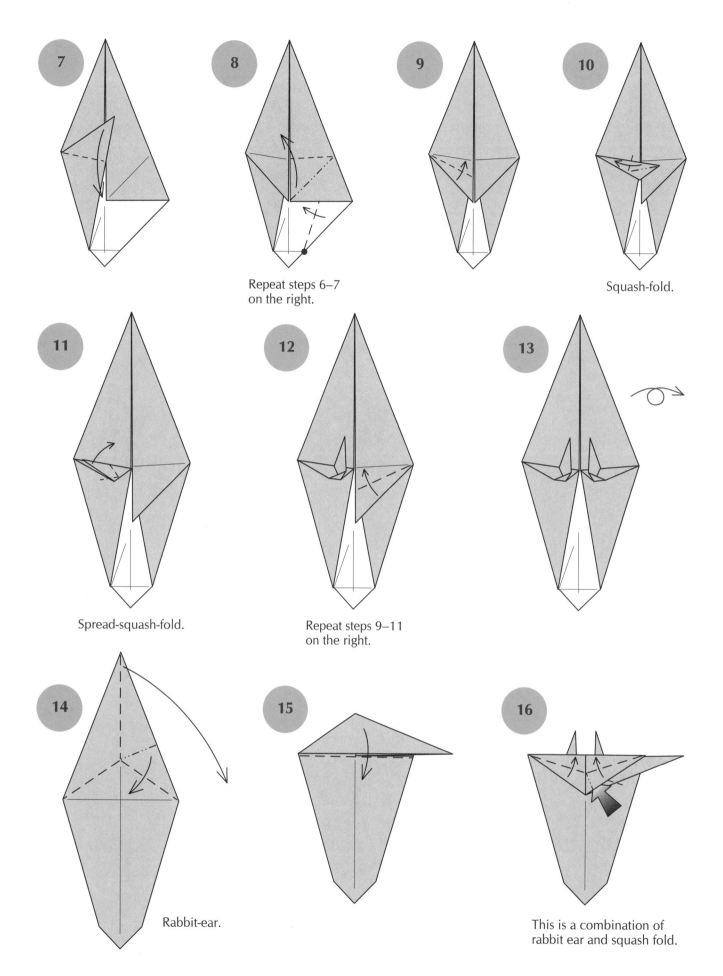

7

8

Repeat steps 6–7
on the right.

9

10

Squash-fold.

11

Spread-squash-fold.

12

Repeat steps 9–11
on the right.

13

14

Rabbit-ear.

15

16

This is a combination of
rabbit ear and squash fold.

17

Unfold. It is best to fold steps 16–17 together to avoid extra creases.

18

Rotate.

19

Fold and unfold.

20

Crimp-fold.

21

1. Outside-reverse-fold.
2. Crimp-fold.

22

1. Crimp-fold.
2. Crimp-fold.

23

1. Fold inside.
2. Crimp-fold.
3. Fold inside.
4. Reverse-fold.
Repeat behind.

24

1. Fold inside, repeat behind.
2. Sink.

25

Pigeon

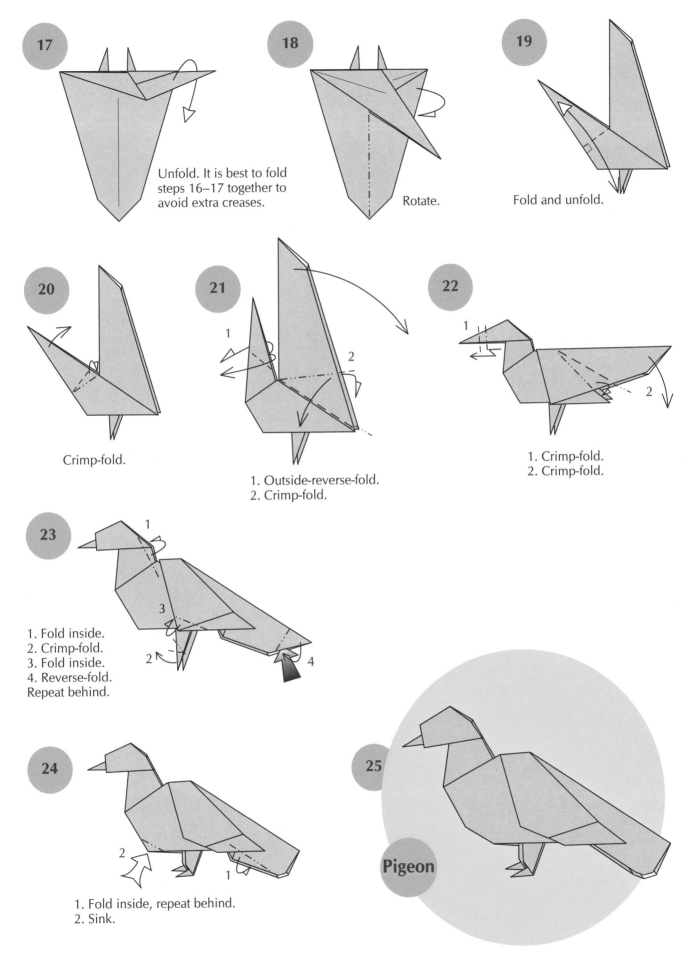

Quail

The quail has a mottled brown, black, and white coloring. A group of quail is known as a covey. It eats insects, mainly earwigs, beetles, ants, and grasshoppers. The quail likes to hide its nest in tall grass and low shrubs.

1

Fold and unfold.

2

Kite-fold and unfold.

3

Fold and unfold.

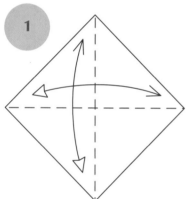

4

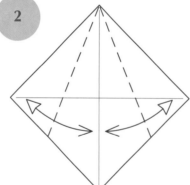

5

Fold and unfold.

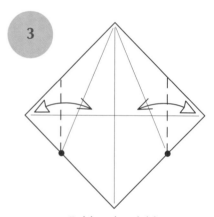

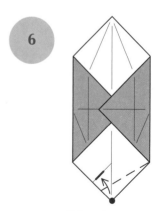

6

Bring the corner to the line.

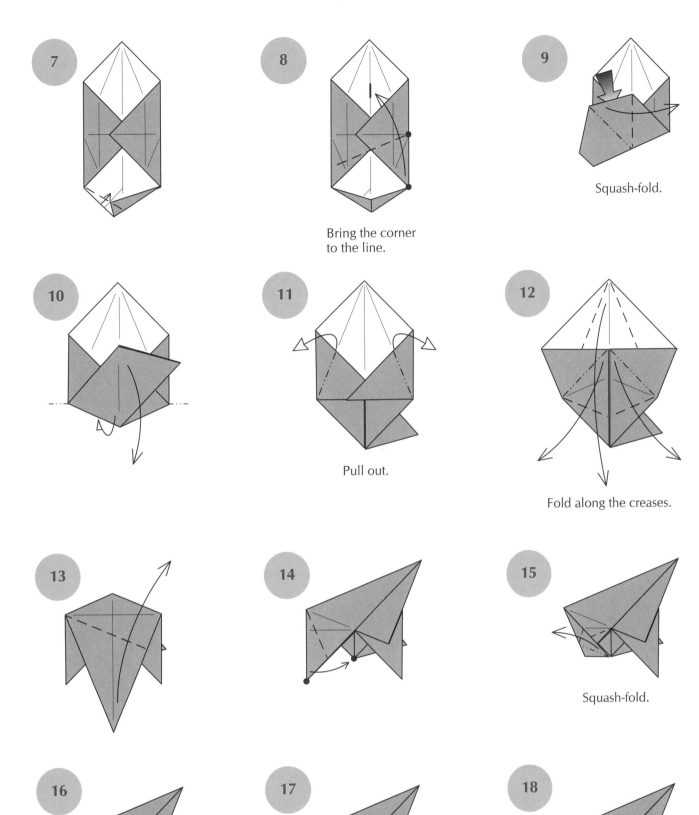

7

8

Bring the corner
to the line.

9

Squash-fold.

10

11

Pull out.

12

Fold along the creases.

13

14

15

Squash-fold.

16

Unfold.

17

Reverse-fold.

18

This is similar
to a petal fold.

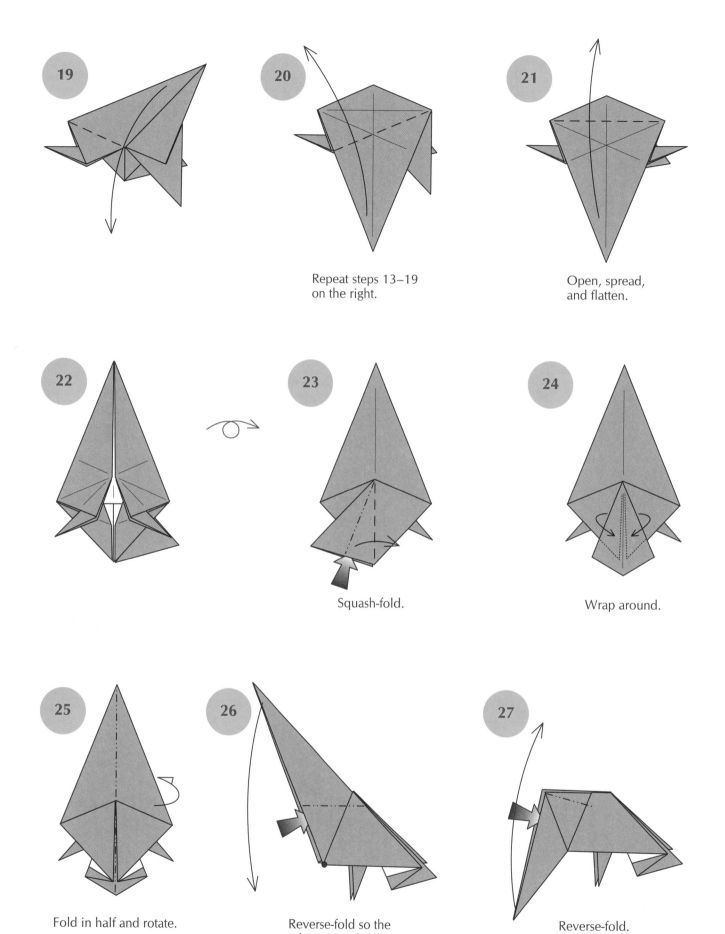

19

20

Repeat steps 13–19
on the right.

21

Open, spread,
and flatten.

22

23

Squash-fold.

24

Wrap around.

25

Fold in half and rotate.

26

Reverse-fold so the
edge meets the dot.

27

Reverse-fold.

28

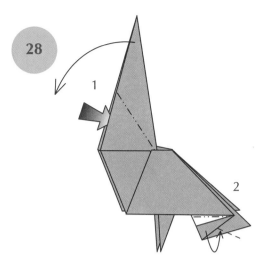

1. Reverse-fold.
2. Reverse-fold, repeat behind.

29

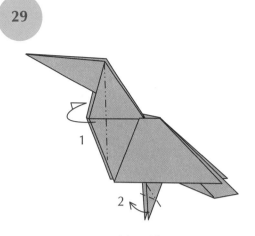

1. Fold inside.
2. Crimp-fold.
Repeat behind.

30

1. Reverse-fold.
2. Repeat behind.

31

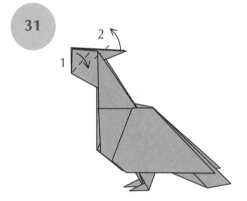

1. Repeat behind.
2. Reverse-fold.

32

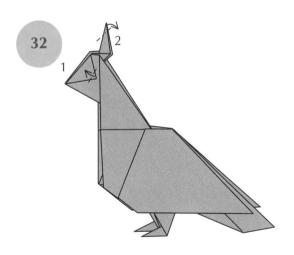

1. Repeat behind.
2. Reverse-fold.

33

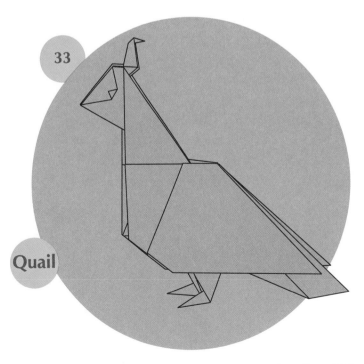

Quail

Roadrunner

Roadrunners are especially fast birds, reaching speeds of up to 17 miles an hour on foot. The roadrunner is usually found in the desert, with its black and white spotted body, and a long tail with tips of white on the end. The roadrunner, unlike most birds, may only fly when it senses danger or is running downhill, and can still only fly for a few seconds. The roadrunner is also the state bird of New Mexico.

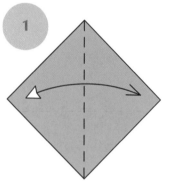

1

Fold and unfold.

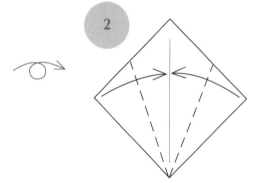

2

Kite-fold.

3

Unfold.

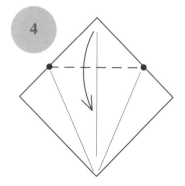

4

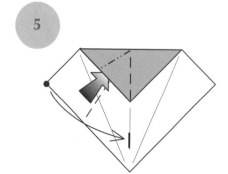

5

Squash-fold so the corner meets the center crease.

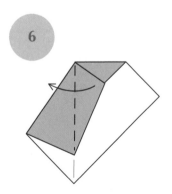

6

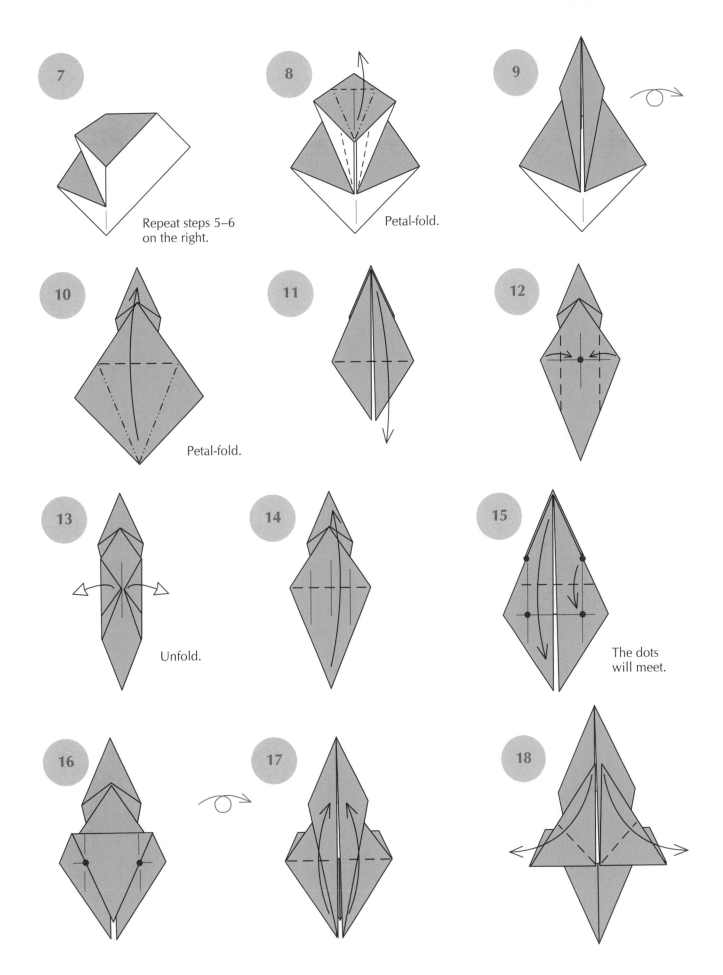

7

Repeat steps 5–6 on the right.

8

Petal-fold.

9

10

Petal-fold.

11

12

13

Unfold.

14

15

The dots will meet.

16

17

18

Roadrunner 111

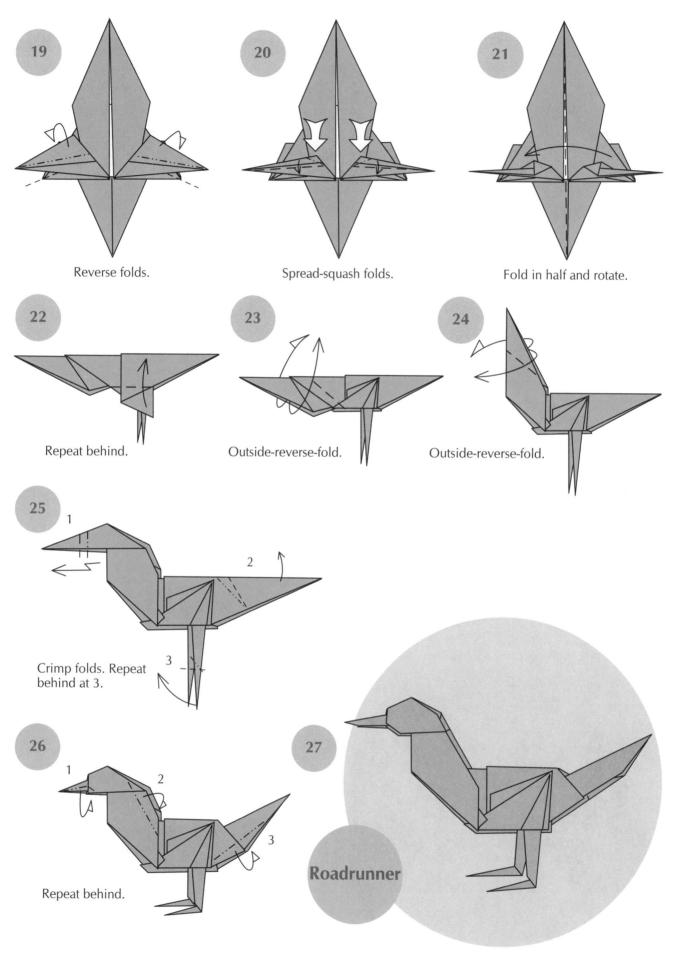

19

Reverse folds.

20

Spread-squash folds.

21

Fold in half and rotate.

22

Repeat behind.

23

Outside-reverse-fold.

24

Outside-reverse-fold.

25

1

2

3

Crimp folds. Repeat behind at 3.

26

1

2

3

Repeat behind.

27

Roadrunner

Stork

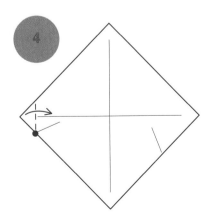

Storks are fairly large birds, between two to five feet in height, which live on all of the continents except Antarctica. Storks are voiceless or nearly so, for lack of a fully developed syrinx (vocal organ), but some of them clatter their bills loudly when excited. Most eat small fish caught in shallow water.

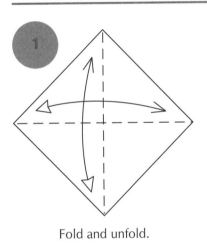

Fold and unfold.

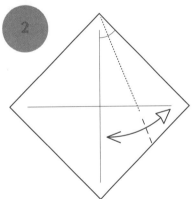

Fold and unfold
on the right edge.

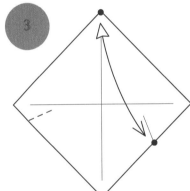

Fold and unfold
on the left edge.

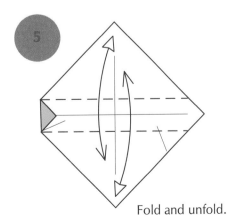

Fold and unfold.

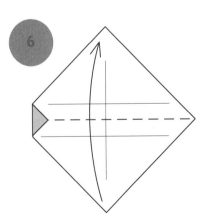

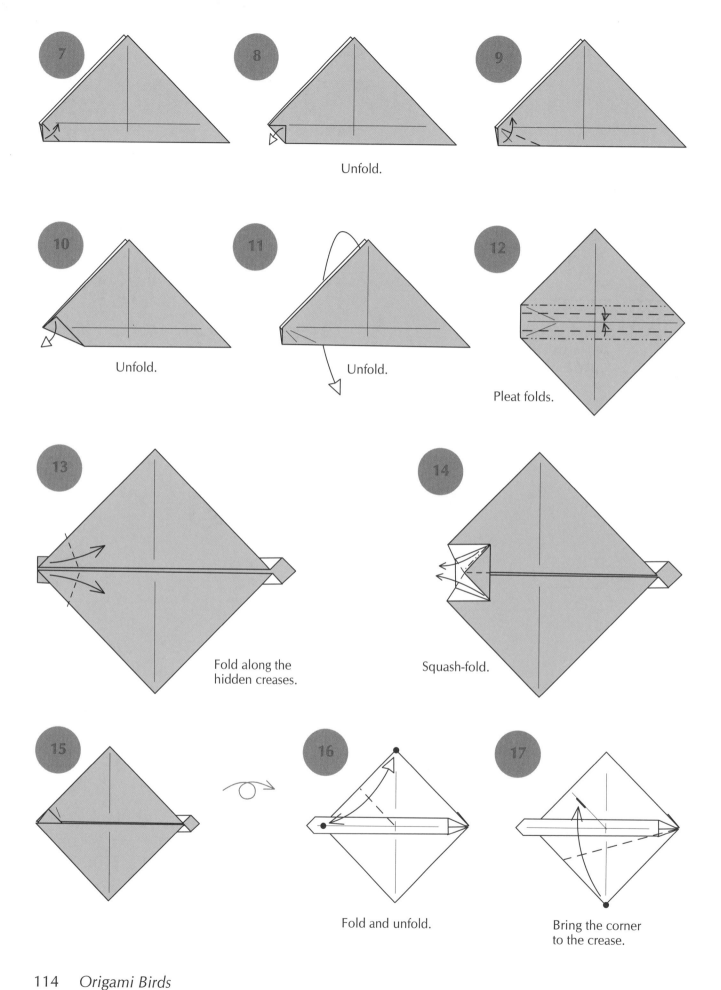

7

8

Unfold.

9

10

Unfold.

11

Unfold.

12

Pleat folds.

13

Fold along the
hidden creases.

14

Squash-fold.

15

16

Fold and unfold.

17

Bring the corner
to the crease.

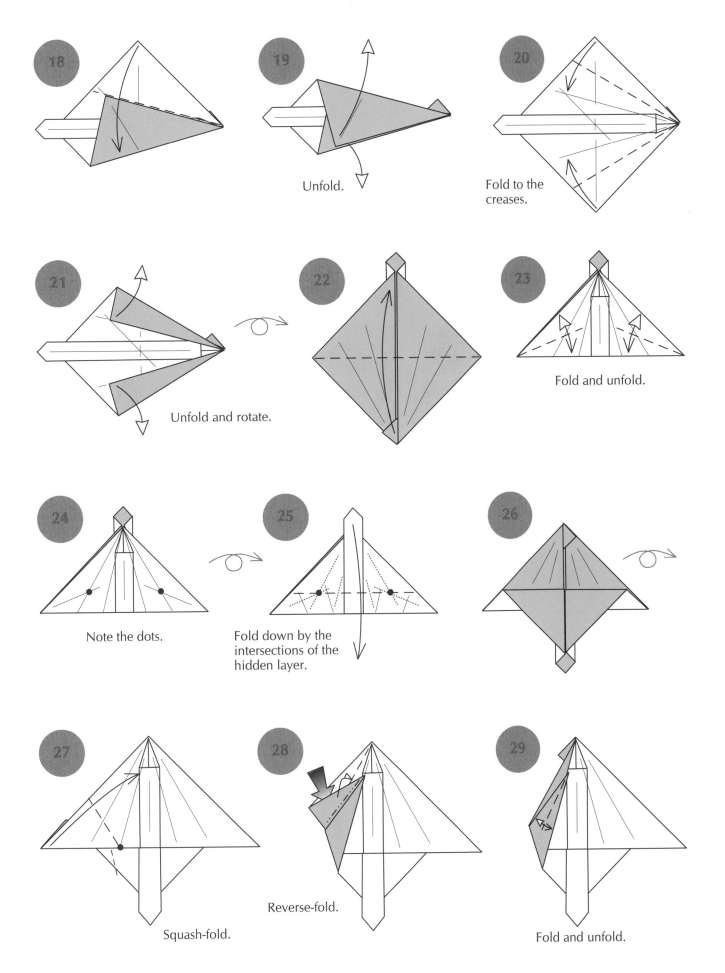

18

19 Unfold.

20 Fold to the creases.

21 Unfold and rotate.

22

23 Fold and unfold.

24 Note the dots.

25 Fold down by the intersections of the hidden layer.

26

27 Squash-fold.

28 Reverse-fold.

29 Fold and unfold.

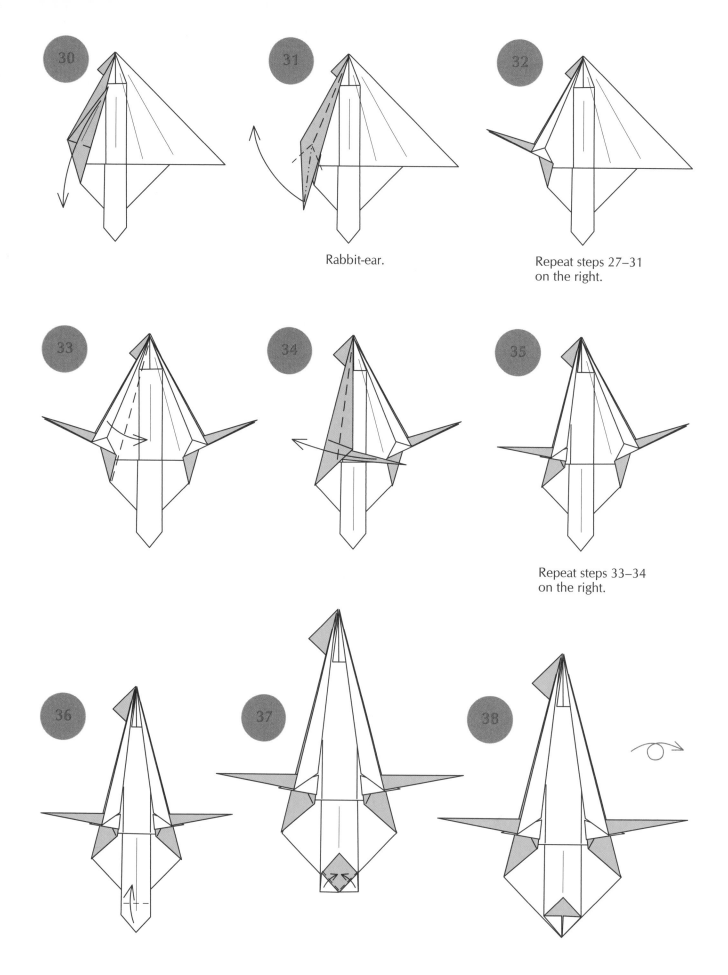

31 Rabbit-ear.

32 Repeat steps 27–31 on the right.

35 Repeat steps 33–34 on the right.

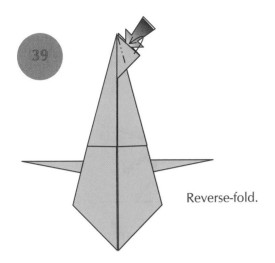

39

Reverse-fold.

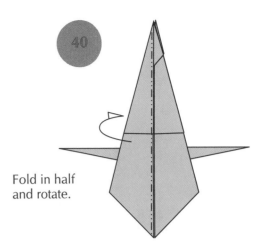

40

Fold in half and rotate.

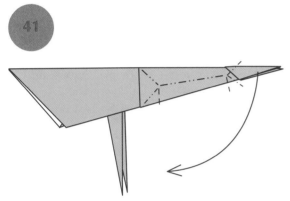

41

Double-rabbit-ear on the left and right.

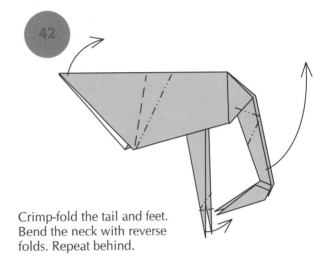

42

Crimp-fold the tail and feet. Bend the neck with reverse folds. Repeat behind.

43

Crimp-fold the tail, thin and bend the legs, open the beak. The stork can stand.

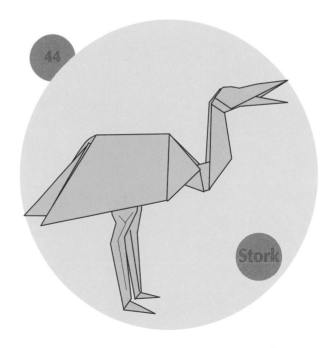

44

Stork

Swallow

Swallows exist in a number of different species and live on every continent except Antarctica. The Cliff Swallows of Capistrano are famous worldwide for their yearly departure from San Juan Capistrano and subsequent return from their Winter home in Argentina. The swallows leave Capistrano en mass and return to Capistrano the same way, and this behavior has become an important part of Capistrano culture, with festivals celebrating their return.

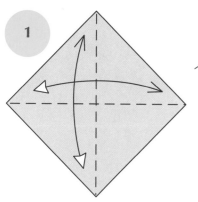

1

Fold and unfold.

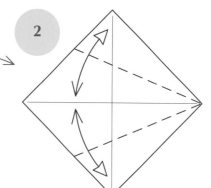

2

Kite-fold and unfold.

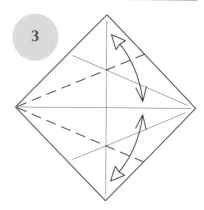

3

Kite-fold and unfold.

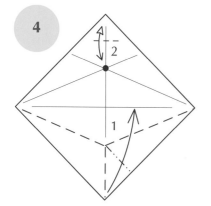

4

1. Rabbit-ear.
2. Fold and unfold.

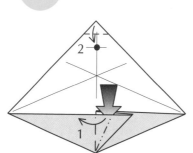

5

1. Squash-fold.
2. Fold to the dot.

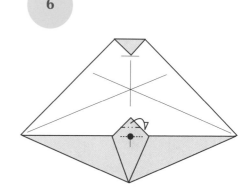

6

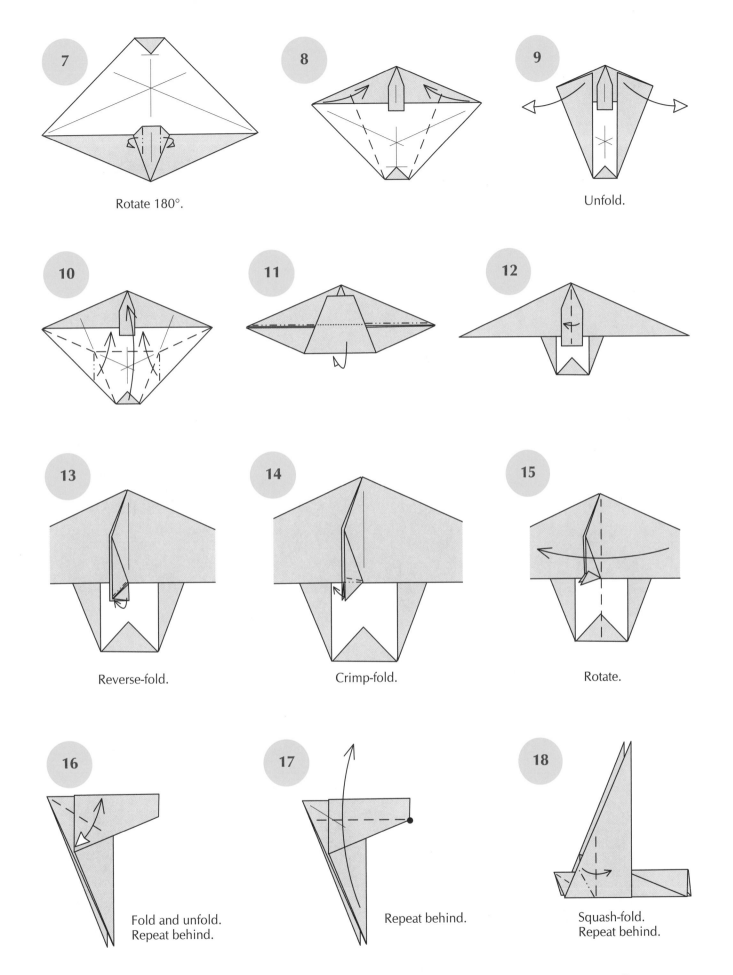

7 Rotate 180°.

8

9 Unfold.

10

11

12

13 Reverse-fold.

14 Crimp-fold.

15 Rotate.

16 Fold and unfold. Repeat behind.

17 Repeat behind.

18 Squash-fold. Repeat behind.

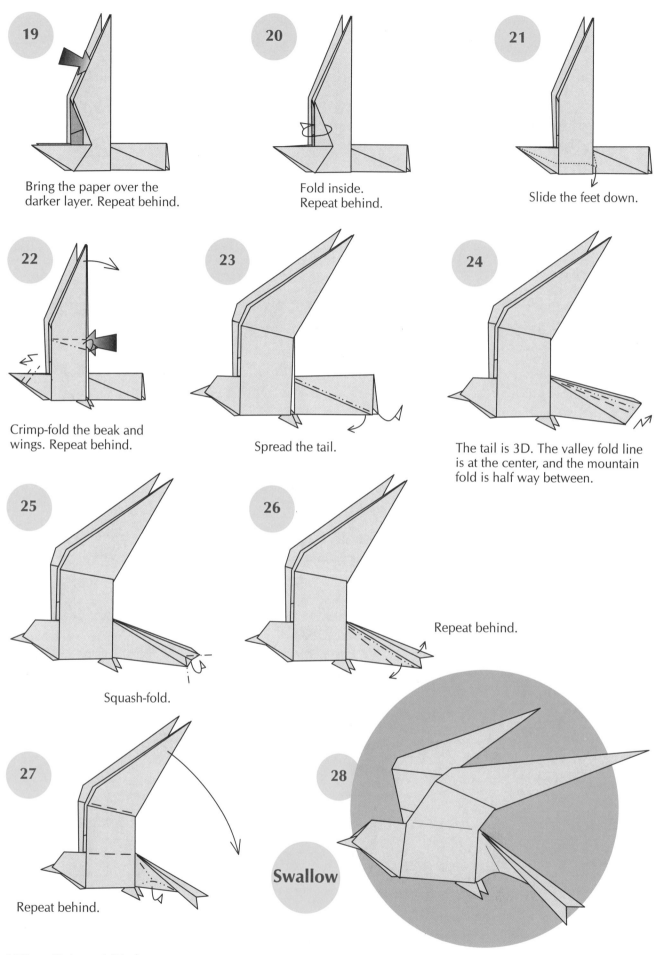

19 Bring the paper over the darker layer. Repeat behind.

20 Fold inside. Repeat behind.

21 Slide the feet down.

22 Crimp-fold the beak and wings. Repeat behind.

23 Spread the tail.

24 The tail is 3D. The valley fold line is at the center, and the mountain fold is half way between.

25 Squash-fold.

26 Repeat behind.

27 Repeat behind.

28 **Swallow**

Swan

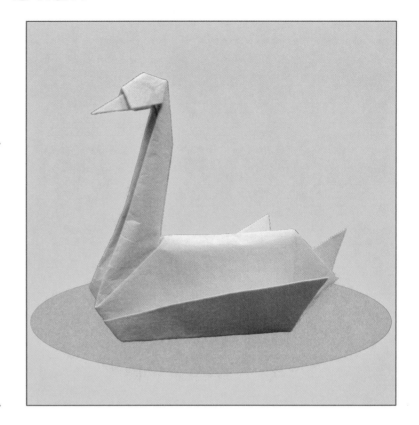

The swan is a large water bird up to five feet long from head to tail. It can weigh up to 22 pounds. It lives in the northern half of the East coast of the United States and around the great lakes. It eats water plants, grain and grass. The swan is very territorial and can be extremely aggressive when its territory is trespassed upon. At a certain time each year, the swan molts all of its wing feathers, making it impossible to fly. Mated swans are able to alternate molting so that one swan can always fly to protect the cygnets, the term given to young swans.

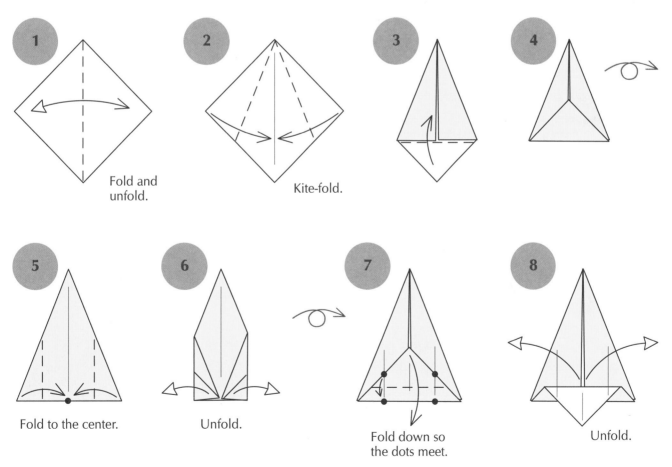

1 Fold and unfold.

2 Kite-fold.

3

4

5 Fold to the center.

6 Unfold.

7 Fold down so the dots meet.

8 Unfold.

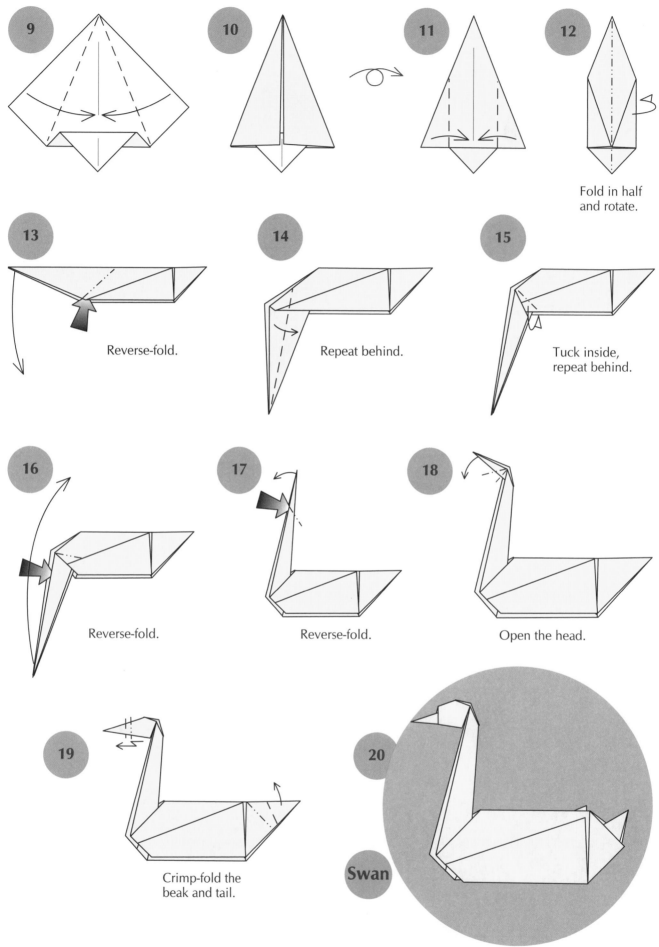

9

10

11

12

Fold in half and rotate.

13 Reverse-fold.

14 Repeat behind.

15 Tuck inside, repeat behind.

16 Reverse-fold.

17 Reverse-fold.

18 Open the head.

19 Crimp-fold the beak and tail.

20

Swan

Turkey

Turkeys are large birds that roam over most of the United States, some parts of Mexico, Hawaii, Europe, and New Zealand. Although most of their life is spent on the ground, turkeys usually sleep on tree branches. Turkeys can weigh between 18 and 37 pounds and eat nuts, seeds, fruits, and insects. Although this animal was almost hunted to extinction, starting in the 1940s scientists reintroduced turkeys into the wild and since then the bird has made a huge population comeback.

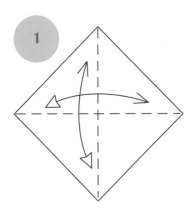

Fold and unfold.

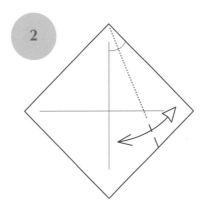

Fold and unfold
by the edge.

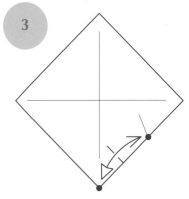

Fold and unfold
by the edge.

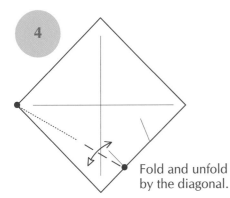

Fold and unfold
by the diagonal.

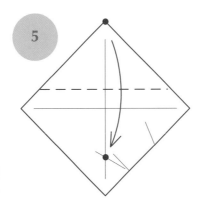

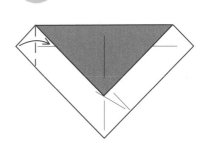

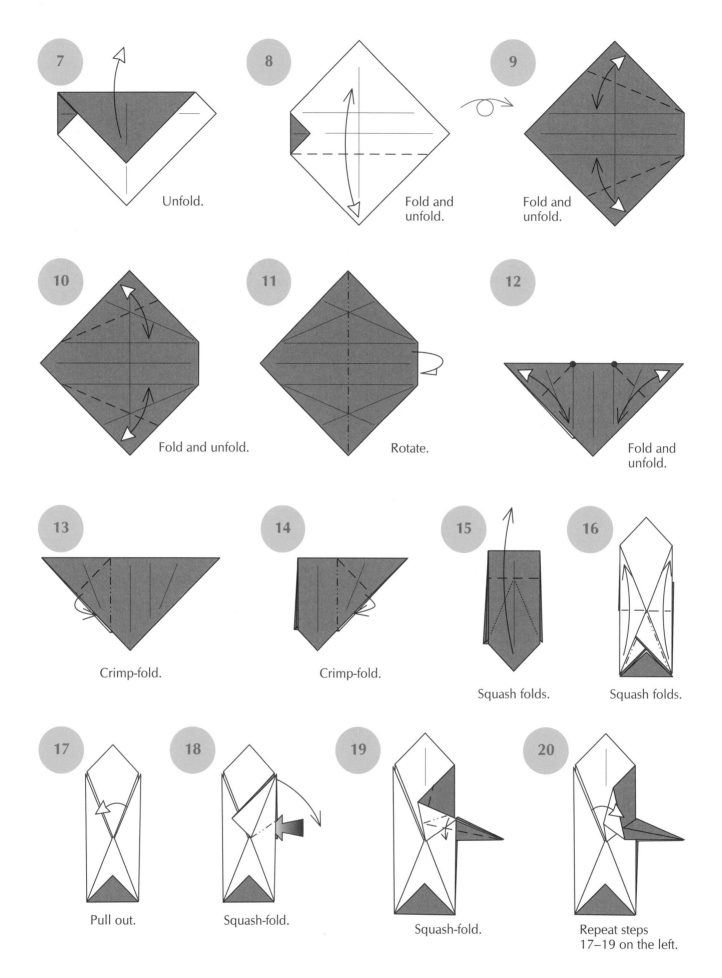

7 Unfold.

8 Fold and unfold.

9 Fold and unfold.

10 Fold and unfold.

11 Rotate.

12 Fold and unfold.

13 Crimp-fold.

14 Crimp-fold.

15 Squash folds.

16 Squash folds.

17 Pull out.

18 Squash-fold.

19 Squash-fold.

20 Repeat steps 17–19 on the left.

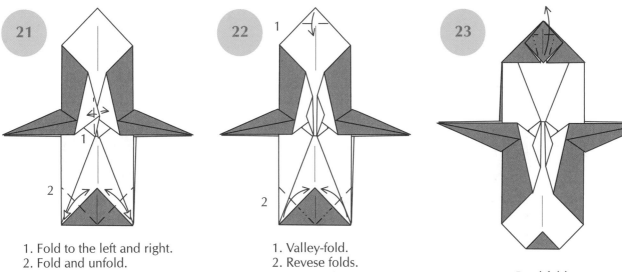

21

1. Fold to the left and right.
2. Fold and unfold.

22

1. Valley-fold.
2. Revese folds.
Rotate 180°.

23

Petal-fold.

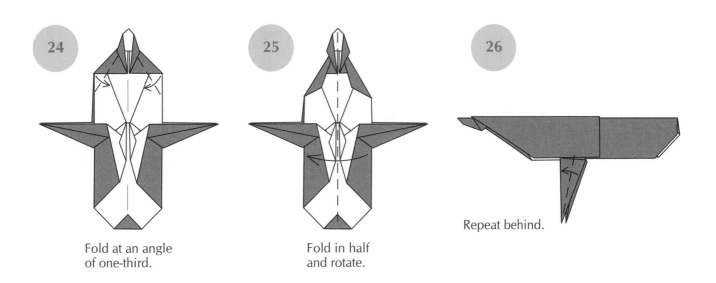

24

Fold at an angle
of one-third.

25

Fold in half
and rotate.

26

Repeat behind.

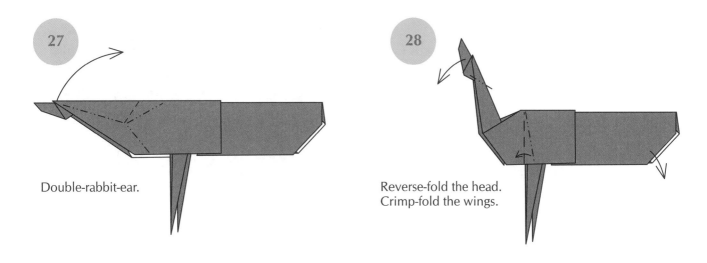

27

Double-rabbit-ear.

28

Reverse-fold the head.
Crimp-fold the wings.

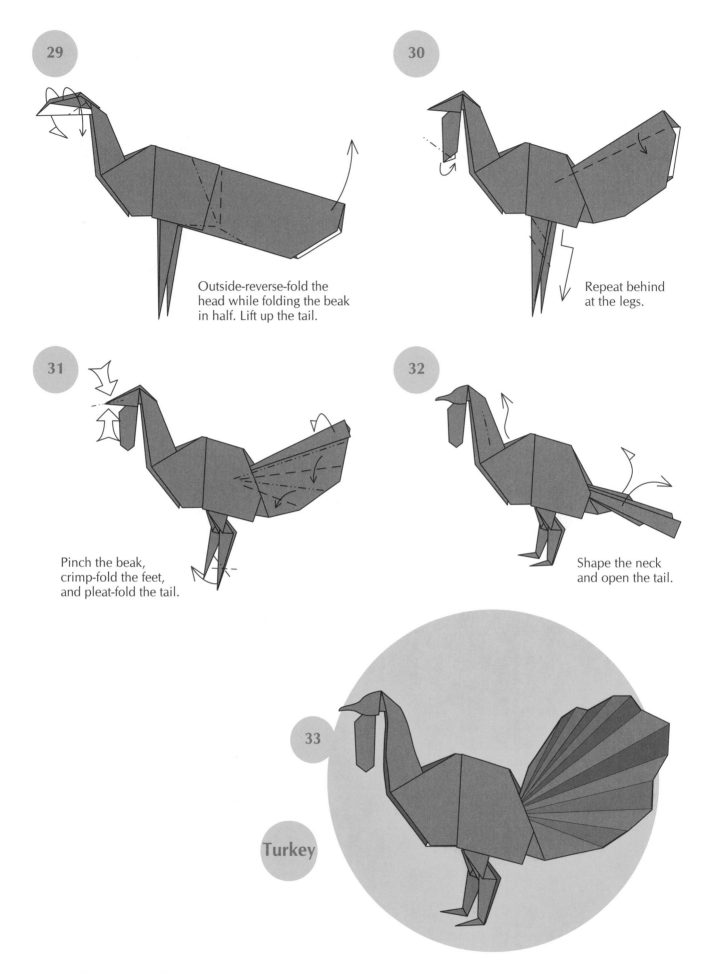

29

Outside-reverse-fold the head while folding the beak in half. Lift up the tail.

30

Repeat behind at the legs.

31

Pinch the beak, crimp-fold the feet, and pleat-fold the tail.

32

Shape the neck and open the tail.

33

Turkey

Woodpecker

Woodpeckers are found all over the world except for Australia, New Zealand, Madagascar, and the extreme polar regions. They are mainly found in forested areas; but have been known to live in treeless areas, as in the case of rocky hillsides and deserts. Woodpeckers are adapted for climbing trees and drilling holes in tree trunks with their sharp beaks. They cling tightly to tree trunks with their sharply clawed feet with toes going both forward and backward. With their long tongues, they can pick insects from the holes they have bored.

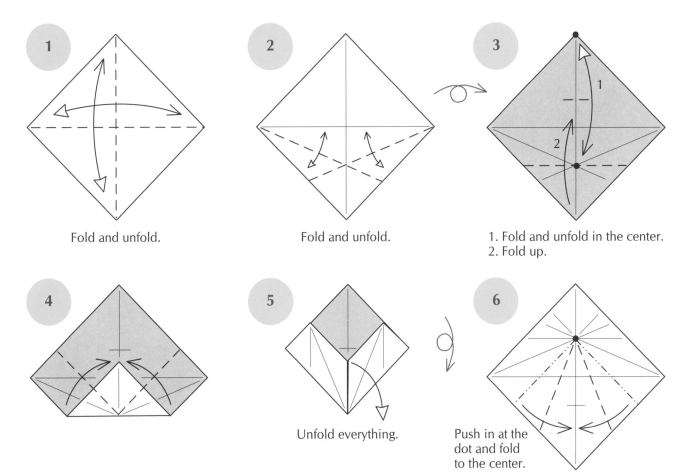

1 Fold and unfold.

2 Fold and unfold.

3 1. Fold and unfold in the center.
2. Fold up.

4

5 Unfold everything.

6 Push in at the dot and fold to the center.

7

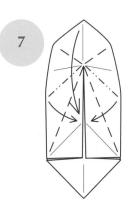

This is 3D. Fold to the center and flatten.

8

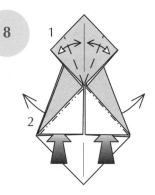

1. Fold and unfold.
2. Reverse folds.

9

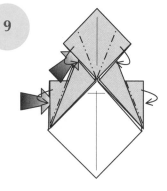

Make four reverse folds.

10

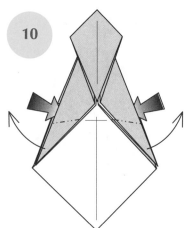

Reverse folds.

11

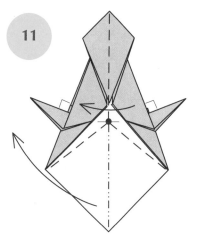

Note the right angles. Rotate.

12

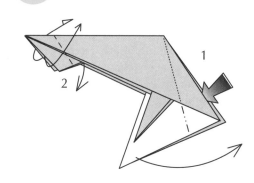

1. Reverse-fold.
2. Outside-reverse-fold and swing out the flap.

13

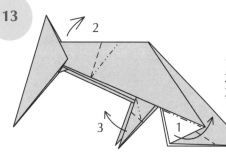

1. Reverse-fold, repeat behind.
2. Crimp-fold.
3. Crimp-fold, repeat behind.

14

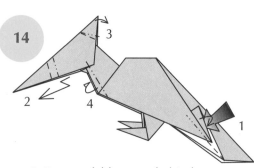

1. Reverse-fold, repeat behind.
2. Crimp-fold.
3. Crimp-fold.
4. Fold inside, repeat behind.

15

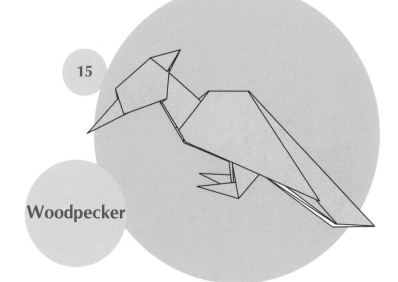

Woodpecker